REVENGE OF A BROKEN HEART

by

T L Phillips

Copyright © 2024 Tina Phillips

All rights reserved. No part of this publication may be reproduced, distributed, or transmitted in any form or by any means, including photocopying, recording, or other electronic or mechanical methods, without the prior written permission of the publisher, except in the case of brief quotations embodied in critical reviews and certain other noncommercial uses permitted by copyright law.

ISBN- 978-1-960853-68-4

Liberation's Publishing ~Columbus Mississippi

REVENGE OF A BROKEN HEART

Finding Beauty in Heartbreak - Revenge of a Broken Heart is a raw, evocative, and deeply personal memoir that pulls readers into one woman's search for love, understanding, and self-worth. The author bares her soul, recounting her experiences with the men who have profoundly shaped her life—both for better and for worse. This is not simply a tale of heartbreak; it is a story of resilience, self-reflection, and an unyielding belief in the power of love despite its many trials.

What makes this memoir so gripping is the vulnerability with which the author shares her narrative. She takes readers through decades, capturing the moments that left her broken and made her whole. The writing is poetic, honest, and, at times, painfully relatable. Her reflections on what love is—and perhaps more importantly, what it is not—are the emotional centerpiece of the book. These lessons resonate deeply, especially when she acknowledges that some agonizing realizations come from understanding that we can mean so little to the ones we hold dear.

While Revenge of a Broken Heart explores themes of betrayal and loss, it does not dwell in despair. Instead, it becomes a powerful testament to healing and growth. The author's unwavering belief that "love is still a beautiful thing" offers a glimmer of hope to anyone who has ever been disillusioned by love. Her story reminds us that even after heartbreak, love remains worth believing in—and striving for.

-USA Today Bestselling Author Angie Daniels

Table of Content

Young First Love 1
Things Changed 17
The Break-Up 33
Big Changes and a Lie 39
The Marriage 55
The Family Friend 69
Living on Autopilot 77
Covid-19 Pandemic 83
Back In Hampton 87
The Return to Maryland 93
Death and Disease 95
Reunited 107
Hawaii 111
The Disconnect 125
Pain and Betrayal 137
Hit Dogs Will Holler 155
Putting Myself Back Together 175
We Reap What We Sow Letters 185
The Takeaway 189

Dedication

To anyone that has ever been a friend to someone that has needed you to catch all of their broken pieces as they fell apart. Your friendship and support were needed so that they could remember who they were. To help them glue themselves back together so they could keep going and move on from their pain. I can assure you that your friendship was necessary and appreciated.

Karina, Daryl, Alexandra, Marie, and Tammie,

It's okay.

I'm okay.

There were sometimes when I knew you were really worried about me. I've come to terms with the knowledge that my love stories did not end the way I had intended or expected them to. I took chances on love but they each fell apart in their own ways and there is nothing that I can do to change the realities of what has happened. I now understand that to be loved properly, someone has to have the capacity and the healing to be able to love me.

I gave my best efforts to them both and I have no regrets. I cannot go back and be the one that was wanted by them. I will be the better version of myself, with boundaries. A version of me that they never knew. Please know that I still believe in love and that love will find me once again. I thank each of you for caring and loving me. In the meantime, I am grateful for the peace of my life along with all of the love, protection and support you each have given me throughout my stories.

My dear wonderful and amazing friends, with all my love, I thank you!

The lack of **respect** was the ***closure,***
The lack of an **apology** was the ***closure,***
The lack of **care** was the ***closure,***
The lack of **accountability** was the ***closure.***
The lack of **human decency** was the ***closure.***
-Unknown

What is a love story?

I don't believe I'm particularly unique in my ability to love those who are outside of myself. I actually believe that loving intensely is the norm for a lot of people. I am one of those people. I love deeply. If I love you, you will never wonder about it. Loving someone is actually a normal thing to do. Most people want to love and be loved. Most of us want to be treated, valued, and honored with respect.

In American society, the romance/wedding industry is a huge business. About 70 billion per year. In which the majority of American girls are cultured and conditioned to aspire to be in love and married one day. Oftentimes, without the guidance and maturity needed to deal with the nuances of relationships, many mistakes are inevitable and bound to happen.

In learning what love is over the years of my life, a main component has been for me to understand what love is and what it is not.

Love is a beautiful thing. I believe in love. These are my experiences with the men I have loved. These are my love stories that have shaped my adult life.

This is mine.

TL Phillips

Young First Love

    I experienced what I believe to be true love at a very young age. Barely out of high school, my best friend Tammie and I leased an apartment together in LaSalle Gardens in Hampton, Virginia. It is safe to assume that at the time, I held a high degree of naivety and immaturity. My friend and I both worked full-time, and I was also a student at one of the local community colleges. At the time, the rent was three hundred and fifteen dollars per month split between both of us for that two bed and one bath apartment with hardwood floors. When I look back on this time, it moved so quickly, and the world was so different then. The funny part is that our money was so tight, it pretty much squeaked! It was me and my bestie coming into our adulthood! We were maturing, learning and attempting to master how to be responsible adults.

    We both were managing our bills but were still so broke that we needed help from our parents on a continual basis. They helped bridge the gap for us between paydays. My mother gave us a couch, and her father gave us a kitchen table set. At any given time, we could go to our parents' houses and get groceries out of their kitchens. They gave us support. Our apartment was a minimalist set-up, but we were grown, paying bills, working jobs, and living our newly adult lives.

I remember hearing a saying as a child. I'm not even sure who I heard it from, but the saying advised people to fall in love with a person's eyes because the eyes never age. A person's body and looks will change but their eyes will always remain the same. I grew to genuinely believe this saying and have carried it with me my entire adult life. I became engaged when I was 19 years old. If anyone ever asks me, "Do you believe in love at first sight?" I will always say yes. That is what I honestly believe. I was graced to meet the love of my life at 19 years old. Many people will say, and did say, that we were entirely too young to be in love. I disagree and have never believed that a person cannot experience true love at an early age. We had true love, and due to our age, it was love in its most sincere, pure form. Times were a whole lot different than what they are now; however, love transcends time. Love is love. I believe I have experienced and known love in its purest, most genuine form.

Across the street from our complex was a McDonalds, affectionately called the "Black Mac" by locals back in the day. This one evening it was late, but I walked across the street and bought some food for a late meal. On my way back to the apartment I heard someone yell out after me. I wasn't sure what the words were exactly, but I turned to look. There was a dark grey car full of guys. One of them spoke to me, well actually yelled at me to get my attention. I think I had nonchalantly waved and smiled, nothing outrageous, then I continued to walk across the double laned street. I had not gotten to the point in young adulthood where I would completely ignore and give nasty looks to guys who were trying to get my attention. I was nineteen and pretty, dressed in jeans and sneakers, and smiling to myself. Nonetheless the driver of the car who had stopped at the light jumped out of the car leaving his occupants there without a driver. He ran to catch up to me as I continued walking. I was startled by his boldness and thought to myself, "This is wild!" And I then got a chance to see really see him.

When I think back, it was at that moment when we locked eyes that I was lovestruck. I saw his smile and his eyes, brown, just like mine. They were warm and friendly. I took his entire face in. His warm, friendly eyes, his great cheeks, his distinct nose, and his super cute lips that were stretched in a wide, bright smile. I was instantly struck by his attractiveness and charm in a way I have yet to experience with anyone else. It was love at first sight for me. I loved him at that very first moment and have every moment since. I knew it then, just like I know it now. It was love at first sight. Even now, when I think of that moment, it still brings joy to my heart. I have known true love, and it started with his smile.

I will try to give you an idea or a glimpse of what I saw, when I looked at this man. Looking into his eyes had always reminded me of a young Michael Jackson, the Jackson Five Michael, Off the Wall Michael before the Pepsi commercial accident Michael. That is My Marine. The man who jumped out of his car because he wanted the chance to meet me. That man who eventually opened his heart to me.

I was flattered by his spontaneous effort. Meeting him this way was spontaneous, exciting, and fun. He made me smile. He made me laugh. I loved him from that very moment. That evening, we stood outside my apartment door for a little while talking and laughing. It could have been ten minutes, or it might have been thirty minutes. I'm not really sure. We stood there until the friends that he abandoned in his car figured out how to find him and picked him up. That night was the beginning of our love story.

I lived in Hampton with my roommate Tammie, and he lived in Norfolk with a roommate. Some of our first dates had been a dinner date to Red Lobster and walking around the Military Circle shopping mall all while talking, laughing, and getting to know each other. Nowadays, that mall is closed and abandoned, and the restaurant is considered for family dinners, birthdays, casual dinners, and the like. It's not so much an impressive first date as it used to be. Due to our age and the times back then, a man taking you for a date at Red Lobster was seen as a big deal, especially with us being so young. In my Sally Fields Oscar-winning voice, "He liked me, he really liked me"! That is what that effort showed. He was trying to impress me.

The next few months had been a whirlwind for us. When we had the opportunity to be together, we were together without hesitation. Weekends or otherwise. Things were good. Really good. We were happy. We were ecstatic! The strength of our relationship was built on us talking and sharing our lives and perspectives. We quickly became each other's closest friends. We had separate lives still, but whenever the opportunity presented itself that we could be together, we were. He kept doing his thing with friends, work, military reserve duty, and family as normal, and so did I with my friends, work, and school. If there were things that he had to do and that I could go with him, he wanted me to ride along. He always wanted me close. That was who he was. So even if it were on Saturdays that he played basketball in the park, I was his tagalong sitting in the car. Since his roommate spent a lot of time out at his own girlfriend's apartment, My Marine would sometimes pick me up to go to his place simply so it would just be the two of us alone. There was a level of bliss that we held between us. The love between us radiated so much that strangers could see how much we were in love. None of this behavior seemed abnormal, obsessive, or controlling to either of us. We simply, continuously were where we wanted to be, which was with each other. Like with anything, everyone doesn't always celebrate or appreciate the joy and happiness in others. Everyone wasn't happy for us. That knowledge slowly crept into our relationship.

My Marine had a lot of family in the metropolitan Washington DC, Virginia and Maryland areas and would visit them often. Although he had several family members in Maryland, including his older sister, he favored his aunt and cousin, so he would often stay at their home while visiting the state. I remember a particular time when he was visiting family in Maryland for the weekend and was staying at his aunt's home. This is way before cell phones for "regular" people saturated daily life. So as soon as he got settled in, he was on the phone calling me. Based on his traveling time and the initial time talking upon his arrival for his visits, I wouldn't hear from him until later in the evening. Possibly 930 or 10 o'clock at night. On this one night when he was visiting his family, I remember this event clearly. It is my understanding that he would sleep on the couch during his visits. As he got settled where he was sleeping, he gave me a call. Within the first few minutes of us discussing his visit so far, I can recall hearing his aunt telling him goodnight. He repeated the good night greeting to me from her and we continued talking and laughing.

As per our usual standard for our relationship, we talked and laughed with each other for hours. We were grown so there wasn't a time limit or bedtime for either of us. Before we knew it, we had been on the phone all night long. It was now early morning dawn. The sun was coming up and I remember overhearing the reaction of his aunt. She said, "Ya'll are still on the phone?" Something else was said but I couldn't clearly hear her. As though the phone had been covered. Then I heard the tension that seemed to come across My Marine's voice after she remarked about us talking to each other on the phone all night. It was palpable. Prior to her entering the room we were in the midst of a conversation. Probably discussing nothing of importance but we weren't about to disconnect the call by any means. We were still both wide awake enjoying each other's conversation. With the shift in the mood, we quickly got off the phone. Later when he returned from this trip, we had a brief conversation about it, but it was dismissed as inconsequential.

This was the first time I got an idea that there were members of his family who didn't care for me too much. This sentiment came up again over time -- that some of his family felt that he was too young to be "as in love" as he was and that they didn't approve. It was only a few members of his family, so I didn't think much of it. From what I can recall from back then, there were clearly two family members who didn't care for me at all, and it was evident to me. My Marine couldn't or wouldn't see it. Whenever it came up in conversation, he refused to believe it and disregarded that he may have family members who showed me any type of slight. From the perspective of some of his friends and family, I had his "nose wide-open." For the most part, everyone was genuinely nice to me, and although I wanted them all to love me, My Marine loving me was all that really mattered to me. I regarded those who didn't like me as inconsequential to what he and I had together. To me, his most important family members were his grandfather and mother. I wanted them to like me because I knew they meant so much to him. It took years for me to understand how important it is to have your partner have the wherewithal and understanding to protect and defend their partner against friends and family members. I didn't know this at the time, but there was a negative influence, and we didn't know it or possibly understand its impact.

After a few months of us dating, his reserve unit was called to active duty for Operation Desert Storm. There wasn't much time to prepare him to go for this mobilization -- possibly a week or so. He had his list of things that he needed to pack, and I was alongside him helping to make sure he had everything he needed. It was a scary moment for both of us because even though My Marine had been "adulting" a little bit longer than me, and he was much better at it, we were still really young. I was scared for him. I didn't want to lose him. The thought of war scared me. I don't remember how quickly it happened or even the specifics of it. My Marine had always been very vocal about what he wanted. This time was no different. During a random conversation, probably in the midst of him going over in his mind all the things he needed to accomplish, he decided he wanted to marry me. So, it was just that simple and then My Marine told me he wanted us to get engaged and then married when he got back. Of course, I said yes! Feeling how I felt for him telling him no wasn't even a consideration. There was no one more perfect in this world than him. At this point in our love story, I loved him, and he loved me just as much. I never doubted the love we held between us. Not only that, but I also trusted and admired everything about him. I saw him as showing bravery and being fearless. My Marine was never scared. He was a hero to me before he had even left for this deployment.

Because of the upcoming deployment, he planned to visit his DC/MD family before he left. This time, the Marine took me with him. Aunt, cousins, sister, other family members but most importantly his grandfather. My Marine really loved and admired his grandfather. When he took me to his grandfather's apartment to meet and introduce me, I was his fiancé -- the one he loved and wanted a life with. My Marine was proud of me, proud of us. He was elated when his grandfather was happy for him too.

Prior to him leaving for the six-month deployment, My Marine bought me a one-carat engagement ring and we set a wedding date to get married for the following year after he returned. He did become anxious about his deployment, unsure if he had everything he needed, but he had a level of comfort and confidence since he was deploying with a few of his good friends in his reserve unit. Even with the challenge of separation coming up, we were optimistic and excited about our future together when he left.

My Marine called from overseas whenever he could and would send me letters. The six-month deployment went by quickly. My Marine trusted me with his finances while he was gone. I didn't recognize how big of a deal that was at the time. I was still incredibly young and still immature in many ways. Financial literacy was one of them. Nonetheless, he entrusted me with his money, and I mishandled some of it, making dumb choices. I didn't do well with this task. I treated his money as though it was bonus money of my own to spend. I ordered magazines and wasted his money! How ridiculous! In the six months he was gone, I should have been able to save a small nest egg, but I squandered his money. Remember I was young and immature. Again, at this time, he was a lot better at adulting than I was back then, and it showed. How I

Revenge of a Broken Heart

managed his money showed how young and irresponsible I was. The money set aside and waiting for him was minimal. My maturity really began improving as a result of the embarrassment and financial mistakes I made during this period. This was a learning experience for us. My Marine was upset and disappointed in me. I had let him down and he was extremely upset about it. He later told me that when I had mismanaged his money during the deployment, that his mother had come to my defense. So, although I hadn't realized it, I suppose she had always been rooting for us to win at life together.

From the outside world, I suppose I looked like I had been much more responsible than I actually was. I was still learning how to be responsible. During this time, I had been working at the shipyard. It was a position I absolutely hated. I was in the Sheetmetal department, and it was a dusty, dirty place that I couldn't get used to. However, working at the shipyard was considered a good blue-collar job. It still is. This job wasn't for me, but as an adult I had to work full-time. My Marine had already been working as a federal employee, and he was happy with it. I am sure he saw that as a level of responsibility that I had, but handling finances was an evolving process. I wasn't good at it. Back then, my phone would get turned off almost every month because I didn't drop it off in the mail. I just walked around with the payment in my bag. Although I was working a blue-collar job, attending community college was preparing me to evolve to get better employment in the future. I didn't want a blue-collar life. It wasn't for me. I knew I was going to be different than who I currently was.

Prior to My Marine leaving on deployment, he had given up his apartment. So, when he returned, we planned for him to move in with me and my roommate, Tammie. When he returned, he and I shared a bedroom, split the rent, and were doing adult things. Initially we picked up right where we left off. We easily transitioned into a regular routine. We worked, I attended classes, he attended reserve duty, and we were living our lives together.

My Marine really didn't talk about his time too much overseas. It wasn't something that came up in conversations, so we didn't discuss it. It was just a blip in our timeline. When he had returned from the war, both of us treated his Desert Storm experience as though it was a business trip. He told me about a few funny experiences he'd had but nothing of shock value. Nothing he ever mentioned was described to me as devastating, shocking, scary, or even "warlike." The way he described his experience with the war was that it was like he was a glorified security guard for six months. After a few months, we found a new place of our own in preparation for us getting married the following year. This place we found was a new apartment development across town from where we had initially met. As a couple we were beginning to evolve. This was a new chapter of our life together.

It was a really exciting time for us. I absolutely adored this man and couldn't get enough of him. We would spend time at home and sometimes go out with his friends to dinner or bowling. We would even visit his parents and siblings while attending church services sometimes. But after only a few weeks of moving into the new place something began to change. We were still young and in love, but as the weeks turned into months something about our relationship was different. My Marine talked to me noticeably less than he used to. The foundation of our relationship had always been our open communication. It was no longer the same. He began doing errands on the weekends without me. Prior to him leaving for deployment, I think the best way to describe us is that we were like magnets. There was a constant pull towards each other. If we were close, we would be as close as we were able and still do whatever was we needed, seldom leaving space between us. It was never draining or exhausting, just a constant pull towards each other.

As fall turned to winter, we began preparing for the holiday season by purchasing a live tree. Having a live tree was a "first" for both of us. It was exciting to have purchased the tree and attempt to get it to stand straight. In the midst of placing the tree in the apartment, My

Marine began itching badly from handling the tree. As he was telling me how badly he was itching on his arms, I reached out and touched his shoulder lifting his t-shirt looking at his arm and I could see red welts developing. As I brought this to his attention, he began itching and scratching even more. The rash from the tree sap was spreading quickly across his arms, back, stomach and chest the more he seemed to scratch. He said, "Go get me some oatmeal, so I can take a bath to stop it!" I rushed out of the house to the shopping center to buy oatmeal. I quickly returned and ran a bath for him. After getting into the tub, the welts and itching still hadn't subsided. My Marine was upset, irritable and itching. I wasn't able to comfort him. As I sat there on the closed commode seat, I asked him, "Do you want to go to the emergency room?" He didn't want to go initially, but we did. When we got to the emergency room, we sat and sat waiting to be seen. Because the allergic reaction was not closing his throat or cutting off his breathing, we sat for quite a while. The emergency to us wasn't an "urgent" emergency from the medical professionals. As we sat there, My Marine was upset and maybe even a little bit hostile. He had nothing to say to me. While waiting there, his rash welts were beginning to go down and the itching subsided. He was no longer itching profusely, but he seemed to be annoyed with me just for being there. An afternoon that had begun with joy and laughter had taken a dramatic turn. Now, our relationship had become different. Something had changed.

TL Phillips

Things Changed

In our new apartment, we lived on the third floor of the apartment building. We had assigned parking spaces, that we were able to directly look down upon from any of the windows. Generally, I returned home from work before My Marine would. I had a closer commute, and I worked the first shift. My Marine would work 2nd shift, but if he worked on a weekend or had reserve duty he would work during the day. Often times I was looking out the window looking forward to his arrival home. This particular day, I didn't see him drive up to the space but when I heard car doors opening and closing, I went to the window. To my surprise, I didn't see him down at his Sonata. On this random day, he came home to the apartment with a brand-new truck. This is what I would consider having been our very first huge blow-up argument. Over his purchase of the Isuzu Rodeo. It was a really cool looking truck. I liked it. Pretty much anyone would have liked it. I quickly put on my shoes and hurried down the stairs so I could see the new truck.

As I quickly made it down to the parking lot to see the new truck, I was excited. My fiancé had a pretty new truck! When I made it to the truck he was sitting in the driver's seat, and I jumped onto the passenger side excitedly asking questions while he was looking through the owners' manual. I told him how nice it was. It was a really cool and modern truck to have. I asked him "How much is the car payment going to be?" When he told me, I was a bit shocked about how much more this was going to cost him. I was a lot more than what he had been paying, and with that I had more questions. All of this was back when understanding negative equity wasn't a thing for us. We didn't really know what it was. Remember we were young. We just knew it made the payments higher and that is what it did. With each question I asked, My Marine was explaining his reasons to me. Becoming more and more agitated with each answer. As the conversation continued, I became more upset with the situation of me not being included in his decision-making process. I left him in his brand-new truck and went back inside the apartment. He remained in his truck for another half hour reading through his owner's manual while I was upstairs in the apartment waiting for him to come in the house.

When My Marine, finally came into the apartment, I was upset that he had made a big-ticket purchase like that without speaking to me about it. He had made a choice without a discussion or even notice of what he was thinking about doing. My Marine wasn't confiding in me, and I took it personally. I continued to ask him questions. "What were you thinking? We're supposed to get married. How can you afford this? We still have to pay for our wedding!" This affects both of us. Every question I asked he had a rebuttal for, a reason he did it. He told me, "It isn't a big deal. I can afford it." It was his money. It didn't matter what I was saying, he wasn't seeing my side. It went on like this for at least an hour. Me questioning him and him defending his decision. From my perspective, we were supposed to be preparing for a life together, which required us intertwining our lives. His doing this was the exact opposite of that. I did know and understand at the time it wasn't a good financial decision. Even though we weren't married yet, it was our plan to be married soon and buying a truck wasn't in the plan or even something we talked about together. I can't say if this was the first time I saw his temper or not, but I do know that this was a memorable experience with his temper. At one point, he asserted himself in the way he spoke and stood simultaneously, and the conversation was over. There was no more discussion about the truck. He said what he had to say, and it was done. The situation was what it was, like it or not. This was the first interaction between us in which the manner that he spoke and how he held his physical stance was indifferent and stoic. Over the next six months, I would see a whole lot more of this temper. This was a side of him that was new to me and new to our relationship. He was easily agitated these days, which would spiral into him getting intimidating and angry very quickly. My Marine now had a zero to ten temper in seconds. I quickly learned that the fastest way to get back to normalcy after something irritated him was to just drop the subject matter causing it. Over the next few months, I understood that to have any resemblance of the loving, sweet relationship that we had together I would have to be leery of how I questioned or challenged a decision that was made. It was important to have a peaceful and loving home, and we had that about 95% of the time. I believed in "for better or worse" way before our weeding date because none of us are perfect.

In our apartment, the second bedroom was unfurnished. Since it was not furnished, we pretty much used it as a catch-all of things and storage. Due to My Marine being a reservist, he would keep his military gear and bags sitting on the floor in that room. One particular week following His reserve duty weekend, I felt suspicious of his behavior. I don't particularly remember why I felt suspicious of him, but I did. So, while he was gone out of the house, I began looking through his military things from the weekend. In the search of his bag, I found a telephone number. Something told me to call the number, so I did. I dialed the number and after ringing a few times a person with a soft, female voice answered the call. I was nervous doing this, but I had to know if My Marine was being unfaithful to me. After nervously introducing myself, I began explaining who I was and why I was calling. I introduced myself as his fiancé and asked who she was to him. The woman on the other end of the line chuckle. As she began talking, she explained that she knew exactly who My Marine was. He had been over at her campus for the weekend. Although getting this information was the reason that I had called.

There were parts of me that didn't want it to be true. The woman on the phone explained that she was a student at UVA, the place of his favorite college athletics. She told me he had visited and come to a game with her and hung out. In the background it was clear there were other people in the room. I suppose due to the exchange between us over the phone, the friends had a grasp of the exchange that we were having. I could hear voices in the background, laughing and yelling "Leave Him!" I'm not sure if they were her friends or roommates. That doesn't really matter. What mattered to me was that they clearly had an opinion of my fiancé and the situation was funny. I found out the information that I was seeking.

I can recall that after getting off the phone with her, I felt hurt and disappointed. I don't even remember the woman's name. I probably definitely blocked it out over time because I once knew it. This cheating incident eventually had become a recurring argument between us. What I found out was that basically on a weekend that he was supposed to be at Reserve duty, he had gotten a ticket to a football game from a co-worker who was related to the student. I didn't have the self-control or the patience to be able to ponder on the information, plan and go forward. As soon as the opportunity presented itself as soon as he came into the house, I confronted him. My Marine was calm and sat down on the loveseat in the living room. As my anger and frustration rose, his demeanor was tranquil. He quietly explained to me that yes, he had cheated on me with this person. Because he was so calm, it shifted the room, and I found myself sitting on the chair opposite to him listening. I wanted to know what he had to say about seeing someone else.

My Marine told me that he had met her for the first time at this game and attended it with her. That it was one time, and he wasn't seeing her or in any type of relationship with her. She had told me as much. My

Marine wasn't lying. He went on to say that he had no intention of seeing her again and that he was sorry. I was told that after the game they went to her room. According to him, she came on to him and he went along with it. When I initially confronted him about it, I wasn't expecting this. It was cheating already because he was in a committed relationship with me and was entertaining someone else. I didn't know he had slept with that girl.

The confrontation I suppose went better than expected because it seems as though he told me everything voluntarily. For the most part, he repeated what she had told me, but he provided me with much more detail. The woman didn't tell me they had sex and hearing it from him was a shock. I had already been hurt that he went on this date with someone else. That was bad enough. My Marine didn't know or realize she had covered for him by not telling me. Learning that detail that he slept with her made me feel emotionally and physically dirty along with the betrayal. Although the honesty can be appreciated, it left me feeling violated. This was a feeling I had never felt before. We argued about this for weeks. For me it was difficult because of the betrayal but for him, he somehow thought that due to him being honest and forthcoming that he had made a mistake that I should be able to easily forgive him for his actions, let it go and move on with our lives.

I don't really know how long it took before I agreed to try to work through this betrayal. I can absolutely recall how much I loved him and still wanted to be with him. I didn't want us to end. I was upset, hurt, and betrayed, but I also didn't want to throw us away. It wasn't about comfort, marriage, or money. I wanted him. Just him. Between the two of us back then, I don't think we made $50,000 combined. The basis of our relationship was about our love for each other and that was priceless. Prior to this cheating incident, we had very open and honest communication. My Marine would show and tell his feelings about things. He apologized and told me so many times, he wanted us. After a while, I was less upset, and I truly believed that he was sorry, and we could get past this betrayal. I actually thought him being so open when he was confronted was a good thing and that it was progress to get us back to where we had once been with our communication. He and I had begun a life together, and neither of us wanted to throw it all away. I loved him, and I wanted to love him for my life. So, I eventually agreed to work through it.

It didn't take much time to pass for another argument to happen. Being young, I didn't know or understand how betrayal affects trust and how you can be fine for one minute and then all of the feelings and emotions come flooding back the next. I just didn't know. This betrayal was really difficult to navigate. I didn't know at the time that neither of us had the emotional maturity to get through this relationship storm.

Not long after the cheating issue, My Marine told me that he wasn't ready to get married and eventually he stated to me he wanted the engagement ring back too. Looking back, I think the span of the chaos that happened once we moved into the Westover Station apartment together was maybe about seven or eight months. As you can probably imagine, this was very hurtful and embarrassing to me with friends and family. We had gone from truly, madly, and deeply in love to not being able to have a conversation without it escalating into an argument. Discussions and conversations didn't help. He had made a decision and was stubborn. So, I knew he would only change his mind if he decided he wanted to. There is nothing that could have been said to change his mind if he hadn't come to another conclusion on his own. Any discussion about it would morph into a full-blown argument. Reluctantly, I gave the ring back, and he stashed it in the ash trash of his new Rodeo. I think I took the ring back once or twice and put it back on. Each time I did that; he got angry and took it from me again.

During this span of time, any disagreement we had become a larger and more huge argument than the last. Complete shouting matches. There was less and less vulnerability, intimacy, clinginess, and communication between us. We were yelling and screaming at each other just about every other day. Back then, I just thought he had a really bad temper -- something I just hadn't seen before he had left for Desert Storm. I know now that he, as well as many other soldiers who served in Desert Storm, suffer from post-traumatic stress disorder (PTSD). Neither of us knew or maybe even realized that the Desert Storm experience was the catalyst that changed him. He was just different. We were different now too. He and I lacked the intellectual and emotional maturity to navigate those changes.

Somewhere in the midst of all of this confusion at home, a fellow student at my community college was consistently trying to get my attention. I knew him as a student from when I was in middle school. We had been in one class together way back then. So, I suppose that he felt an ease in approaching me, as though he already knew me. When people talk about the importance of keeping peace in your home, it is for reasons such as this. I can now look at that experience as though the classmate was lying in wait, like a panther to attack our relationship at its weakest moment. My relationship wasn't strong anymore. I had never been a cheater before, and I have never wanted to be. Being sneaky and underhanded doesn't come naturally to me. Being a cheater and liar seems to require time, effort, and energy that I didn't want to give. That isn't my personality. I am a serious relationship type person that believes in love and loyalty. When I'm in, I'm all in.

During this time in the relationship with My Marine, I wasn't getting the same love or attention at home. It wasn't like it used to be. My Marine didn't want to be my fiancé anymore. I wasn't being loved like I was once being loved, and I felt alone. Despite having shared with the classmate that I had a man at home and that we lived together, he was persistent -- surely due to our age. I'm not sure what young guys are like now, but back then they would try really hard to get a woman's attention. Not staying in the relationship with My Marine was never a consideration for me until I felt the further embarrassment of my relationship.

On this one particular day when I had an evening class, My Marine had dropped me off. This wasn't the norm. I usually drove myself to classes. I can't figure out why I wouldn't have driven in consideration we both had our own vehicles. So, it is possible we had been out together and had run out of time in order to get him home and me back to class in enough time. I was dropped off in front of the school and I proceeded to enter. After my two classes were over, I went outside. The weather was nice still. Cool enough to have a jacket but comfortable enough to be outside for a while without getting cold. When it was time to be picked up it was already dark when I went out and My Marine wasn't there waiting for me.

After standing outside for about 15 minutes, my former classmate walked out of the building. He saw me from a distance and as he passed by, he said, "Hey. What's up?"

I stated, "Nothing much. Just waiting for my fiancé."

I volunteered the information that he had been on his way. To make it seem as though I hadn't been standing out there waiting unsure of when he would arrive. With that explanation, my former classmate walked on to his car in the parking lot. When he got to his car, I noticed he didn't turn on his car and left. He sat in his car. I'm not sure how long the former classmate sat in his car watching and waiting before he pulled off with me still standing out there waiting. I stood there very self-conscious and aware that my fiancé had me standing outside waiting for a ride. I was outside in front of the school standing there about 45 minutes before he arrived.

The next time my former classmate saw me at school, he said to me, "cut that zero and get with a hero." The classmate was a veteran too, so this was purely a veteran-to-veteran insult. I would hear this from him again on several occasions. I found this to be embarrassing to hear. I couldn't defend being left standing outside at night. Someone had witnessed first-hand that I wasn't a priority in my live-in boyfriend's life. I felt shame.

It had gotten to a point where I looked forward to going to school because that guy was interested in talking to and being near me. I didn't have that at home anymore. Home consisted of quiet, disagreements, and arguments. I didn't trust My Marine anymore and we weren't doing well. So eventually, I let the guy from middle school be nice to me and show me attention. The former classmate and I would sit and talk between classes in the school break room. Not because I had a great interest in him, but because things were not good at home, and it was nice to have someone who actually wanted my attention. On one hand, I had a hell-raiser at home in which things just didn't seem to be meshing between us anymore. On the other hand, I had a classmate who was always really nice and expressed his interest in getting to know me better if

I would only give him a chance. I enjoyed the attention. My Marine and I were still a couple, but our intimacy had changed, and we were no longer engaged to be married. Our future wasn't clear.

Both My Marine and I were raised in the church and our families would invite us to church services, events, and gospel concerts. So, our faith was an aspect of our lives that was at the forefront of our lifestyle. It was also a glaring reminder that we weren't married. At this point, it wasn't in our plan because we no longer had a plan and were now just "living in sin."

My Marine still liked to be socially active and hang out with friends and do things on the weekends as though nothing had changed between us. We wore masks to the world. I was still very introverted during this time and primarily spent my time at work, school, home and with My Marine's friends and family. One weekend we went bowling with his friends. My Marine was an athlete. There was virtually no sport that he would do or try that he couldn't become great at with just a little bit of effort. I was never great at bowling, so my time was focused on talking and chit chatting with one of the wives or girlfriends than it was on actually bowling. So often times, the ladies would sit further back to the side since our focus wasn't really on the lanes or the scoring.

As I was sitting in the lane chairs talking, I looked up and saw the fellow student from the community college come towards our lane. He walked directly to the table and chairs directly behind our lane and sat down. When he and I made eye contact, I did not speak. I only turned my head as though I didn't see him. He didn't say anything to me, us, or anyone in our group. He just sat there for about 10 minutes. Just watching. I don't know if My Marine ever noticed, but I did. Although I hadn't cheated or done anything or went anywhere with my classmate, I had enjoyed the attention and conversations at school from someone else. It made me uncomfortable, and I felt guilty even though there had been nothing going on between us. I was wrong. Following that weekend, I began avoiding the classmate whenever I saw him at school. That little bit of laughter and fun at school wasn't going to be worth a two-to-three-hour battle if My Marine ever found out.

Although I loved My Marine and wanted to be his wife, he said he didn't want that with me anymore, and it was weighing on me. That bowling alley stunt from the classmate had me shook. I didn't want to be accused of cheating, and I definitely didn't want to bring any unnecessary anger from My Marine my way. Our home life was chaotic and toxic already. I couldn't bring anything more into it. By this time in our relationship, our disagreements were full blown arguments. Yelling and screaming was a part of our regular dynamic between us. Sweet looks and cuddles between us became fewer and fewer. If something wasn't resolved quickly, it created more questions, distrust, and more animosity between us. If an argument wasn't going My Marine's way, or if he felt he was done discussing it, he was fine with getting in my face to be intimidating. I had been a co-worker and classmate to people who lived with domestic violence in their lives. His behavior began to scare me when he got enraged. He wasn't the same guy that used to be soft and vulnerable with me. Our relationship had become intense and dramatic,

The Break-Up

During this time, all talks and discussions about marriage would lead to an argument. So, I stopped talking or asking about it. He didn't love me like he used to. There was nothing in how My Marine spoke to me, regarded me or treated me that could influence me otherwise. I was now convinced marrying was no longer an option for us and the commitment was just shaky. At some point, I told My Marine I was going to move out since we weren't getting married anymore and we shouldn't be "living in sin." I told him we would still be a couple, just not living together. At first, he didn't seem to care and was completely okay with it. Then in maybe a few days or a week, he changed his tune. He wanted me to stay, which he tried to convince me of. He was trying to date me and spend time with me again. We were back to going to dinner alone, even walking the mall like we did when we first started dating. I can recall with all the convincing that he did, he never said he wanted to get married like we had originally planned. He just wanted me to stay in the relationship and the apartment. I think I left when there were about two or three months remaining on the lease, I moved back home to my mother.

Here is the reality of the situation: I lied. I lied to him about why I was moving out. When I moved out of the apartment we shared, I knew I wanted our relationship to be over. It was no longer what I wanted, and it had gotten so volatile and toxic between us. I knew I loved him, but he wasn't loving or nice to me and I definitely wasn't his priority anymore. We weren't happy and we weren't friends anymore. Our relationship had changed, and I wanted to get out of it. I was young and fine. I was okay with being single.

When I first moved out, we initially kept in contact, but the emotional distance remained the same. I visited him a few times when he moved out of our shared apartment and moved back to LaSalle Gardens. At first, I was really sad about the break-up. I spent my nights and weekends renting movies from Blockbuster video. I'd watch two or three and go back to get a few more. I stayed to myself. I think at first, he enjoyed the space and freedom until he realized I was creating that space. There were a few visits when we would meet, or I would go to his new place that was great for us and then there were also visits where we just couldn't get along. Then I stopped visiting and communicating with him all together. It then changed to him coming to visit me several times at my mother's home. He became more and

Revenge of a Broken Heart

more persistent over time. It had gotten to the point where I was telling him to "move on" and that I didn't want to talk to him anymore or even try. I didn't want to keep doing this with him.

I decided to begin dating again. This was a period of time in which if someone asked me if I would like to go out with them to lunch or dinner, my response would be, "I can eat!" I began going to lunch, movies and dinner dates on a consistent basis. There was one time when I left out of the house to go meet someone for a meal at Denny's. When I jumped in my car, the engine kept choking out, and I couldn't get it to start. I tried several times, and the engine just would not start. My sister's boyfriend at the time, Pat, drove up about the same time as I was outside and parked about 10 feet back from my car. When he got out of his car, he walked up to my driver's side window. He said to me that there was fabric in my tailpipe. This honestly had scared me. Immediately I knew it was done by My Marine. Who else would have done it? He had stuffed the tailpipe of my car.

Pat walked around to the back of the car, kneeled down and pulled the fabric out of my tailpipe. When I cranked the key in the ignition again, this time the car started. I went inside and was talking to both my sister and her friend. Knowing the temper My Marine had, I thought he was trying to kill me, and they agreed. Within a few hours My Marine came by which allowed me to confront him. When he arrived, the yelling started almost immediately and I expressed, "You're trying to kill me!" He tried to assure me that he wasn't. He said, "I was just trying to make sure you didn't leave before I could talk to you." I can't say if I believed him or not. By this time, I had become physically scared of him and what he might do. He had never been violent towards me, but he would be intimidating or behave threateningly during arguments when we had lived together, to end them. Because of that, I thought he was unpredictable even though I was also angry he was trying to control me, and we weren't a couple. We had a few exchanges like this. Our dynamic had already changed. We were off track, and it seemed as though we couldn't and wouldn't ever be on track again. I can say in retrospect, he kept trying to talk to me, so he could try to convince me to give us another chance. For whatever reason, although I still loved him, the desire to rekindle the relationship wasn't there, and I didn't think it was coming back. I still had a high fear of his temper and couldn't trust him. I needed space and time. I loved him, but I just couldn't do it anymore. Eventually, he stopped pursuing me and stopped coming by unannounced. He had moved on.

For about six months or so after leaving My Marine, I was in a pretty bad car accident hit by a drunk driver. My sister's boyfriend, Pat, was also a friend of My Marine from the reserve unit he served with during Desert Storm. Pat told My Marine that I had been hurt, and it prompted him to visit me during my recovery. I hadn't seen him in months. When My Marine visited me at my Mother's it was unexpected. Due to the accident, I was limited to sitting and having to lay in bed during my recovery. I was only getting up to go to the bathroom. When he came into the bedroom I was surprised to see him. I was also happy to see him. It was a really nice visit. There was no pressure from him and no discussion about rekindling our relationship. I was happy to see him. This would be one of the last times I ever saw him. At this very moment in my life, with everything that I am, that has been done and said, I still love My Marine. I will always love that man. I recognize now that the love we shared had been the measure I compared everyone else to.

Big Changes and a Lie

I took some time to myself and after a few months of recovering from the accident, graduating from community college, and accepting some random dates, I began talking to that classmate on the phone and going out with him. He was really good looking, had a nice body and was the only person that I had met that seemed as though they had a genuine interest in me as a person. He was funny and I enjoyed being around him. We had gone out for a few months and began dating exclusively. It didn't take much time to figure out that we didn't have anything more than shallow conversations and jokes. We just never clicked on a deeper level. The chemistry between the classmate and I just didn't meet my expectations or was even comparable to what I had before. He wasn't for me, and I knew I was still in love with My Marine. The relationship between the classmate and I was done, and I was completely fine with that. So just about as quickly as it began, it was also over.

Early 1994, a couple of months after ending the short-lived relationship with my former classmate, I realized I was pregnant with my first child. When I found out it was still early in the pregnancy, so I knew I had options.

Within a matter of hours of finding out the news, I told my former classmate about the pregnancy. He was calm and not very reactive. He softly asked me, "What do you want to do?" I told him, "I have a full-time job, a car and am responsible so it makes sense to be responsible for my actions." I can't say if he particularly agreed with me or not, but he chose not to give me his opinion on what I should or not do. What surprised me was him asking about trying our relationship again. I cared about him, but I wasn't in love with him. I knew I didn't want to be with him. I wasn't really interested. I had a lot to think about and eventually I made the decision that I was responsible and accomplished enough to bring a life into this world as an unmarried woman. After several more talks we decided we would co-parent. I also had a supportive family so I knew that I would be okay.

I remember as clearly as yesterday; I was about four or five months pregnant. I'd already had my first few prenatal check-ups. This was following my 23rd birthday. It was late and I was lying in bed, and I missed him. I became overwhelmed to tears. I missed My Marine. I had thought to myself how I wish that things could have been different. I missed the love we had shared and how much I wished that this was our challenge to face together. I remember thinking to myself, that I wanted My Marine back but now it was too late. My Marine and I weren't planning to have children. He had been adamant about never having interest in being a foster parent or even adopting. It would have always been us with the exception of my Godson and any nieces and nephews. I remember thinking that even if I wanted to try again, there was no way he would want or accept me now that I was pregnant. I was about to be a Mother, and I was scared, but all I wanted to do was to talk to him. He wouldn't be able to see me at all now that I was pregnant with a child. He would only think I was coming back because I was expecting. I remember crying that evening. Not because of the fear of what I would be facing but the reality of cementing the end of all possibilities of that relationship rekindling. He wasn't coming back, and I wasn't going back.

This is when my backbone began stiffening. I had to be strong. There were no other options for me. This is when and why my maturity and true independence began. No matter if I was ready or not, I had to become solid for not only myself, but my child.

During a routine prenatal exam in May, I was advised by the doctor that my blood pressure was elevated. I had chosen a female doctor because I had felt as a woman she would always be a better choice. During my previous visits I had seen her partner in the practice, and he had never mentioned that each visit my blood pressure rose. This time, my doctor advised that I needed to check into the hospital so that I could be monitored more closely. I have never had a male OBGYN provide me care since this time in my life. After checking into the hospital, my pressure was noted at 250/110. I had my daughter as a preemie in May at 24 weeks by emergency C-section. She remained hospitalized until she reached four pounds, about four months later.

A few months later, in early fall while at my Mother's house, my sister and her boyfriend, Pat were at the house. This is way before social media like we know of it today. Myspace might have been around, but gossip was primarily limited to face-to-face and telephone calls. Like most people, they wanted to hold my baby. As Pat was holding my baby, he asked me had I heard about "My Marine." The answer of course was no, I hadn't heard anything about him or from him in a really long time. Almost a year by this point. With a sparkle in his eye (maybe not, but that is how I remember it), he told me that My Marine got married to someone else. The way I remember this; he had a smile or possibly a smirk on his face. It was as though it brought him pleasure by telling me this news. I pretended as though it didn't really matter to me (I am sure I shrugged my shoulders) because he and I had moved on with our lives without each other. I was pretending so I wouldn't show the pain on my face. It did matter to me. It hurt. I can't lie.

All at once, the memories of what we once were to each other and all of the regret came rushing back in. Over the next few times I would see Pat, he would always tell me about My Marine's great new marriage -- some update, news, or a tidbit about his life. When I thought over our relationship and engagement, how it ended and how quickly he married someone else, I was even more hurt and offended. Over the years I came to believe that he just didn't love me as deeply and honestly as I had loved him. I couldn't fathom that he could have possibly loved me the same and was able to marry someone else so soon after our break-up. When it came to our then impending marriage, he seemed so serious about it that he wanted to wait. So, I had no reason to think he thought less of marriage now. With us, nothing moved fast. Either he really didn't love me, or it was a rebound/relationship marriage to have that level of commitment with someone else. Eventually, after a few years I came to terms with this and accepted it as my reality. His marriage and new wife was not a rebound.

The information that I had been given about his first wife was that she was quiet and more reserved and strait-laced than I me. After hearing that I felt I wasn't a good girl or saved enough. After self-examination I concluded that she was a more ideal young woman than I was. And when I saw her for myself, I could tell she was different from me. Although I considered myself to be a "good Christian" girl. Her image came across even more sheltered, withdrawn, and quiet than I was. So, in my mind, since he then chose her and did go through with the marriage with her, I hadn't been those things. That is why he didn't marry me. That feeling haunted me for years. That feeling of not being enough. I was mad and furious at him for not loving me enough and at her for having the life with him that I had wanted.

I internalized all of these feelings and did what a lot of women do when they don't feel like they are quite enough. I began to make myself more in the ways that I could control. I began my undergraduate degree in Human Relations at Trinity in Washington, DC a few months later. Even though I was the one who chose to leave the relationship, there was a level of emotional trauma that I had to unpack and deal with when trying to understand why he didn't love me enough to want to marry and build a life with me. For a while, I didn't feel like I was "enough" and that was the reason that My Marine did not choose to marry me. The Marine was my first true love. I have never doubted that. Because we were so young, I also think it was pure love in its greatest form, even though it didn't work out.

Over the next few years, I focused on raising my daughter, getting educated, and loving myself as a person and single parent. Like many people in their twenties, I worked a full-time job, hung out with friends on weekends, and was busy navigating how to become a productive adult. At one point, I had a job with a collection agency but got laid off. Being a single parent and sole provider while living in a two-bedroom apartment was financially scary. I didn't make a lot of money with that position, so the unemployment checks barely covered anything outside of the primary necessities.

This setback is why I chose to join the US Air Force Reserves. It would create a financial back-up plan if I ever were to be laid-off again. I did find a position at a call center fairly quickly, but I knew I had to be sure to always have enough. So, I took the ASVAB (Armed Services Vocational Aptitude Battery) exam, which is to determine qualifications for the miliary, interviewed for an intelligence position at the unit and scheduled my bootcamp dates.

When single parenting, the time seemed to fly by. During those early years, I tried to figure out why he didn't love me enough to marry and build a life with me. This soul search of what went wrong with this relationship and what was wrong with me that he couldn't love me, led me to begin dealing with my own self-doubts and recognizing I had some lingering abandonment issues. Throughout my twenties, I thought of him less and less, but the measure of how I viewed what love was supposed to be, remained the same.

Over the next five years after having my daughter, I felt as though I was suffocating in Hampton. It felt as though I was evolving, and I no longer fit within the city limits. I couldn't be the newer, better version of me in Hampton, and I wanted out. Joining the USAFR created more options for me. I figured it was a good part-time gig to have while getting myself together financially. By the time I left for basic training, I had been at my full-time job long enough to be eligible for military leave of absence. So that's what I did. I was gone for a little over three months while my mother cared for my daughter. When I returned from training, I continued raising her, working my regular full-time job, and attending reserve duty on my assigned weekends.

Revenge of a Broken Heart

Hampton Roads is a military area. There is Navy, Marines, Army, and Air Force men throughout. So that was a large part of the local dating pool. Although I had dated a few military people since having my daughter, I refused to date a Marine again under any circumstances, but Navy, Army, and Air Force were fair options. Shortly after becoming a reservist, I met the man who would eventually become my husband during a duty weekend in Delaware. When I began dating my fellow reservist, I had been single for a little while. I had decided that I wasn't going to date "a type," only someone who was nice and that wanted a serious relationship too. I wasn't going to focus on any superficial qualities. There was no "he has to be this, that, and the other." That is what I got. He wasn't as tall or as heavy as I preferred, but he was nice, and he was interested in a serious relationship. It was by no means perfect.

I met him during Reserve Duty weekend on Friday night while I was out at the Dover Non-Commissioned Officers club. When his friend introduced him to me, I had noticed he was already a little tipsy. I have never been a drinker and wasn't raised in a "drinking" household. For that matter, most of my friends were barely social drinkers. So, I really didn't know what being drunk looked like. But no judgment. I let it fly. There were big similarities between us and those things are what I gravitated to. When he was introduced to me, I was told his regular job was as an attorney. That night he asked me to attend a retirement dinner with him the next night. So, I went, and we had a really nice time. I was willing to see him again. I was really excited to tell my cousins about him. For a regular single-parent working woman, the opportunity to date an attorney would be an upgrade. I was beginning a professional career and that is the type I wanted for a partner.

Unfortunately for me, on Sunday he said there was something he needed to tell me. Guess what it was? Yes. The Fellow Reservist wasn't an actual attorney. He worked at a law firm as a contractor at the time. The truth was that he had done law courses in college but didn't finish that path. That was a huge disappointment. I continued to talk to him because he had the honesty to reveal the truth right away and not continue to mislead me. So, we continued dating long distance.

With the Fellow Reservist in Washington, DC and as a single parent in Hampton, a long-distance relationship wouldn't be too far or too difficult. At this point in my life, I was used to adulting and being responsible, and even though he was a parent of a son, he wasn't as responsible as I was. In many ways, I think I overlooked many of his shortcomings due to assumptions that he was more responsible than he actually was. This became a huge issue over time. Prior to him and I beginning to date, I had been planning a solo trip with my daughter to Disney World in Florida. I had been planning and working on this trip for months before I got involved with him. When the Fellow Reservist learned about my plans, he asked if he and his son could join us. There was no reason to refuse the company, and I shared the planning information, so that he and his son could join the trip. About a week or two prior to the planned departure date that summer, I found out he had not completed paying for the trip costs for him and his son. When I shared the frustration with a girlfriend of mine, she recommended that I disregard it as a "mistakes happen" situation, since he was scrambling to handle it so that they could still attend. This was the first experience in which I was able to see financial irresponsibility.

Once we began seriously dating, I decided to accept a position in Washington, DC and moved away from Hampton to Burke, VA in January 2000. Initially, I temporarily left my daughter with my mother, so I could find a place for the two of us. I found and bought a small condo in Burke. That summer, I moved my daughter into our little 2-bedroom condo. It was a fresh start and a new chapter of my life in a new town, in a new place, with a new job, and a new man.

After dating for about two and half years, the Fellow Reservist hadn't spoken about a future life with me. When I asked him about future plans for us, I found there were none. I had honestly come to the realization that I could end the relationship with him, start dating again and get married more quickly than if I continued this relationship with him. I thought maybe we weren't a good match after all, and I began to feel as though he wasn't serious about me. As a result of me continuously feeling this way about this relationship we in fact broke up. I was completely fine with this. I was so through with dealing with him, I don't even know how long we weren't together. Feeling how I felt, I had no regrets. However, I know I was completely okay with being single again at this point.

During a reserve weekend, he caught up with me outside of the military commissary going to my car. The Fellow Reservist wanted to talk to me. I wasn't motivated to go talk anywhere else, so we talked and had a long conversation right there in the parking lot. During this conversation, he stated that he wanted us to get back together as a couple. I suppose I kind of was looking dismayed in the face because he then said that we could get married. In retrospect he was placating me by saying what he thought I wanted to hear. So that is how I was "proposed" to technically. No bended knee. No grand gesture. Just that we could get married. The Fellow Reservist was now my Future Husband. The upcoming Christmas, my Future Husband came to Hampton for the holiday and presented me with a ring in front of my family. Immediately we began planning a wedding for May (five months out) to be held in Washington, DC at my university's chapel.

As I have gotten older, I have grown to understand, listen to, and interpret the voice of God. I'm sure I don't always get this right. None of us do. But I am better at it than I used to be. Definitely better than I was at this point in my life. In all transparency, I recognize there were signs about many things that I didn't recognize at the time as red flags in the relationship that would later be huge issues within our marriage. In retrospect, clear signs that we probably shouldn't have gotten married. Signs about money management, alcoholism, accountability, faithfulness, responsibility, and family dynamics. These things that I ignored and definitely overlooked during our dating life and leading up to us getting married, should have caused me to pause. It should have had me focus on some of those issues that would or could develop into problems. Signs and red flags. I ignored every last one of them. Not knowing and understanding signs or red flags when they present themselves has been detrimental to me personally and mentally over the years. Hindsight is often 20/20.

The following February as a USAF reservist, I received mobilization orders for Operation Enduring Freedom. This became the first major conflict that personally impacted me and my new fiancé. The conflict was caused by me asking him to take care of my daughter when I left for the active-duty mission. Without hesitation or a reason, he refused and said he couldn't do it. Me being upset is an understatement. I was furious at how little he seemed to care about me or what my needs were in this situation. My initial reaction to him was questioning how he can be a fiancé/husband or parent if he wasn't willing to take care of my child during my absence.

To me, this was a fair question. To me, marriage meant that you stand in the gap for your partner if need be. You fight for, defend, assist, and protect your partner the best way you can. After this huge argument (and me throwing a picture frame across the room), he agreed to take care of my daughter when I left for the mobilization. His unwillingness to try to help me without prompting was a red flag that I chose to ignore. It had been my opportunity to question what kind of man was willing to be my husband but not willing to step in to be a father to my child when I had a clear need. I never thoroughly asked myself this question of why there was a hesitation. What I had needed happened, so there was no reason to dwell on the negativity of it. I moved on. His caring for my daughter was short lived because unfortunately, within three weeks of me being mobilized, he received orders for mobilization too. Luckily, my mother was able to temporarily relocate to Burke to provide care for my daughter for the remainder of the school year. In retrospect, I see that I have tended to "move on" from things without fully assessing the why's, how things have happened, or even the possible ramifications of whatever the episode or incident long-term effects could be.

Over the next few months, the logistics of being on active duty in Delaware, ensuring the logistics of my daughter's care, maintaining my primary home, and attempting to create normalcy while trying to still plan a wedding were daunting. I probably should have just postponed the wedding or just called it off. I remember that a former co-worker mentioned this, and I completely bulldozed over the suggestion. Years later, I have always wondered what she saw that made her suggest that.

Thinking back, I realize I felt the pressure to get married and establish a strong family unit. Being a single parent has never been glorified in American society or religious communities, and I definitely felt that societal pressure. Being from a Christian background, I didn't want to do what many single parents do when they move to a new area and lie that I was widowed or divorced. I have always wanted to be my true self. Unapologetically. Being a liar is not who I am. For my child. I would do most anything for their safety and security. Marriage often can create that. Society isn't kind to single parents, and I wanted her to have all of the love, advantages, and support she would need to develop into being a great adult. Although my Future Husband was technically a single parent too, the mother of his child carried the primary responsibilities of caring for their son several states away.

The Marriage

My Future Husband and I married in May 2003 in Dover while on active duty for Operation Enduring Freedom. It was a full-fledged wedding -- white dress, tuxedos, limousines, and a reception with an open bar. It was a nice wedding. I don't regret having an actual wedding instead of a courthouse marriage. I believe we loved each other, but I was aware our love was different from my previous love story. I knew that although I wanted a loving and affectionate husband that wasn't what I had. We checked the boxes we each had of what a suitable marriage partner would have been. I had a husband/partner who would eventually lead me into becoming a married single parent. I believed at the time he loved me, but I don't think he was ever in love with me. I would be told this much, years later.

There is a difference between loving and in love, and no one will ever be able to convince me otherwise. There were many things that I rationalized when I stepped into this marriage. Things that I knew were important to me or things that I knew I wanted that I wasn't going to get. Unfortunately, there also were a great deal of things that I didn't and couldn't have ever predicted.

The relationship between My Husband and I was never very close. In retrospect, he and I weren't friends. We were involved. We had been a couple. He and I didn't have the type of relationship that included hugs and holding hands. The bar for our level of vulnerability and intimacy was very low. He had told me early on in our relationship that holding my hand was uncomfortable because for him at 5'8 and me at 5'7, he considered me too tall. I wasn't small and delicate I suppose. The average American woman is 5'3. I'm considered to be tall in most settings. If I am wearing high heeled shoes, I am a giant. That was one of those red flags that I overlooked. This was a way for him to reduce an expectation of intimacy and affection. General affection wasn't a part of our relationship.

In some ways, it is possible that we did check off boxes for each other, and in other ways we did not. However, some of the things that I looked over at the beginning, developed into things that I craved and longed to have in a relationship. Again, I did love him and recognized that when we married, being madly in love was not our reality. I settled with not being "in love." If we sat in church or a function, he never wrapped his arm around my shoulders. That wasn't our relationship. There was seldom any affection between us in public or behind closed doors. As time went by, there were less and less vulnerable or intimate moments that would cultivate that type of closeness between us.

At the beginning of our marriage, we lived in Dover, Delaware while I remained on active duty. My husband's orders ended after six months, but mine were extended. In the midst of this, My Husband returned to work commuting back and forth to Washington, DC as a manager for one the largest telecom organizations in the country.

During the time I had been on active duty, I was saving enough money to ensure that I could pay all of my personal bills and car note while remaining unemployed during the first year of our second daughter's life. About a year and a half after getting married, we welcomed our youngest daughter into the world and moved into our home in Upper Marlboro, Maryland. Looking back at the whole of our marriage and what is likely common in many marriages that end in divorce, our best times were our first few years together. In favor of keeping disruption in our family down, I chose to let my contract as an Air Force reservist expire since My Husband already served in the USAFR for well over a decade compared to my six years. It seemed to make sense for us not to risk both of us ever having to be mobilized simultaneously again. So that is what I did. I did not renew my military contract. I considered this as an act of love and dedication to my marriage and family. Beginning September 2004, I became a stay-at-home mom with no outside employment. After a little while, getting to the one-year mark I realized I wasn't ready to go back to work outside of the home. So, I got the idea to start an in-home childcare business. I did the research, took the required courses, and applied for licensing and inspections. Once I was cleared, I began working full days with before and aftercare school students and two babies, in addition to our baby, while still maintaining the home.

Over the few years when we were in Delaware, I had realized that my husband's drinking was a concern. If he went out with friends, he returned more than tipsy on the weekend. After marriage, I realized that I wasn't aware of or even understood his drinking while we were dating. As someone who was raised in a household in which there was no one drinking, it never was an issue to me that people would drink socially. That is what I thought My Husband's drinking was when we were dating. Strictly social. I can recall that my stepfather was a drinker, but because he had married my Mother after I graduated from high school, I wasn't familiar with any type of "drunken" behavior. I soon learned that drunkenness is more than slurred words or even passing out. It wasn't a behavior that I knew growing up at home and it wasn't what I would see with my friends as an adult, so to see it in someone that was this close to me was a foreign experience.

When My Husband and I were still dating, I can remember a specific reserve duty weekend in Dover when his friends had brought him to my hotel room because he was drunk. They didn't want to leave him alone, so they brought him to me. That was the first time that I had ever seen someone literally standing in front of me while simultaneously moving in a circle. Before this time, I cannot recall ever being so up close and personal to someone that was drunk. I had friends that drank, but nothing like what I was experiencing and seeing firsthand in my marriage. Because of my lack of familiarity with alcoholism and drunkenness, I really thought that had been an isolated incident. More of a fluke. I came to learn and understand that my husband drank to get drunk every time.

I learned that for some individuals, it is the love of the taste or the effects of the alcohol that they are unable to stop. Over time, I came to learn that alcoholism likely increases with time. In the case of the eighteen years in which he and I were married, there was more and more drinking over the years. It took a while for me to learn and understand this. What I originally thought seemed like weekend drinking evolved into daily drinking. I've learned rationalizing or making deals with an alcoholic doesn't work and recovering/rehabilitation has to be wanted by and be a priority for them for it to be effective. I would say that the drinking during the early years was primarily on the weekends or when he was out with friends. If he had been drinking, it was more likely than not he would be drunk. My Husband's alcoholism evolved over the years. This is something I didn't even realize was a possibility for a future reality for my life.

During this period of my marriage, it was very important for me to be a good wife and a good mother. That was my primary goal. At least I conducted myself according to what I had believed at the time was to be a good wife and mother. I suppose that one day, I'll get a critique and feedback from my children on how well or poorly I did.

In the early years of our marriage, household duties were all mine. Cooking, groceries, cleaning, laundry, and ironing were all me. Even the scheduling and emotional duties of raising children were my primary responsibility. Being a stay-at-home wife and mother was the hardest work I had ever done in my entire life. It was extremely important for me to be good at it. It was 24 hours a day, 7 days a week with no days off. Although I wasn't working outside of the home, childcare was and still is a lucrative business to own. I was easily able to give My Husband $250 a week in order to contribute to the household bills.

This period as a stay-at-home wife and mother was the only time I have ever been provided for financially by my husband in which he maintained the primary household bills during our entire marriage. I'm not complaining about that, because all adults should take care of the debts they create. It is also a fact that many men have no interest in being a provider. The 50/50 thinking is a common occurrence with the 21st century American man. Throughout my entire marriage I never felt protected or covered financially. I have always had to be careful, cautious, and prepared with money for the "what ifs." I learned with time that if there were ever financial hardships my husband was not a resource for me to turn to. I came to learn that when I walked into this marriage my Husband wasn't good at all with managing money. There were signs prior to marriage, but I would just move on and not dwell on the problem when it seemed to be resolved. I hadn't paid any attention to them. When hardships came (and they always did) either I would have to figure it out, wait it out, or in cases where it was crucial, I would have to reach out... to my family members and try to borrow money. This of course was an embarrassment for me, because asking an uncle would surely get a question as to why My Husband couldn't get the money or at least be the one asking for the loan. In all honesty it was a fair question. I myself have asked that question whenever a family member reached out to me for financial help. A husband should be leading the family in all things, at all times.

During the first few years of our daughter's life, I worked from home keeping my business until she was in the K-5 class. I then slowly transitioned back to working outside of the home. Initially it was part-time, then on to full-time. Those five years of working from home and the dynamics that happened throughout that time cemented dynamics in our marriage that we were never able to shake or get past.

Throughout the entirety of our marriage past relationships that I shared while we were dating seemed to be an ongoing threat to the consistency of our marriage. Even high school relationships were a trigger. It was so bad at times; I can recall going into a box of my old pictures and memorabilia to find that some pictures were completely gone or had been cut up with the faces removed. The average person would consider this a form of jealousy, but it didn't end there. Any relationship failures or insecurities that I shared with My Husband would be thrown in my face somehow to demean any success or gain I had. As with any relationship, individuals reveal their successes and failures of past relationships. There were some particular men from my past that he would repeatedly bring up throughout the entire marriage. There was a high school guy that I dated briefly after high school that My Husband had cut the faces out of old pictures.

A football star that I knew from high school, My Marine, The producer that I dated prior to dating him, has never met any one of them. To my knowledge he had never seen them. Yet, throughout my marriage, I would hear unprovoked venom about those four men. Over the years, My Husband refused to attend any of my class reunions. His reasoning was, he didn't "know any of those people." My Husband had never met anyone of significance from my past with the exception of family and close friends. He had never experienced any type of threat to our relationship. In fact, in Maryland, I had no close friends or family.

As I had mentioned to you previously, this caused tremendous stress on my self-worth. Whenever an incident occurred, I blamed myself and doubted myself. I wondered what I could have done differently to bring about a better result. I started a behavior of self-analyzing and doubting who I was throughout the years and wondering if I was attractive inside and out. I came to believe that I was not attractive enough, and it became a part of my core being. There is truth in saying, whatever you hear often enough, you start to believe. You see, I have always thought I was a pretty girl. I had been a popular cheerleader in high school. After high school, I dated men who thought and considered me to be "fine." There was never a shortage of men trying to get my attention. Any time someone would complement My Husband about my attractiveness, he always laughed it off. According to him, if I had been more attractive, he would have done more and spoiled me more.

With the passage of time, working from home, getting older, body changes from pregnancy, and self-neglect, my view of myself changed. I didn't know if I was still "that girl." I was married to someone who would take the time to tell how much I wasn't "that girl" every time he had the opportunity. Once he had the audacity to tell me what My Marine would and would not have done. He even ridiculed our engagement. My Husband told me on more than one occasion that My Marine would have never married me and that I was lucky that he had, me being a single parent and all. I was told so many times that if he hadn't married me nobody else would have. I wasn't fine enough. He even told me that if I was fine, he would have done anything for me. As I am sure you can imagine, we did not become closer through the years, only more and more distant.

One would think as a married person any external validation would commonly come from your spouse. I didn't have that. I was seldom given any compliments. My only validation was from myself and over time even that ceased. I didn't receive Valentines, anniversary, or birthday gifts, and I seldom received Christmas gifts. My Husband didn't think I was great and after a while, I began to believe him. Looking back throughout my twenties and thirties, my face card was only declined by me. The self-doubt had set in. My Husband was my judge and jury.

There were some pleasant times throughout our marriage in which we would be able to get along and behave as though the bad things didn't keep happening. All of those good times or moments were short-lived. He always circled back to making sure I knew I was not what he wanted in a wife. As if he was what I wanted in a husband. Even so, I can confidently say I never got the impression that My Husband would ever leave me. I was likely safe and secure in that. No one wants to start over, and unfortunately, both of us were comfortable being in an unhappy marriage. So, life kept living.

As the years passed, being a good wife was not a priority to me anymore, only being a good mother. I loved being a mother, and I was doing everything within my power to provide as stable of a life for my children as I could. That included trying to maintain a two-parent household. I had closed my in-home daycare and was back in the outside workforce. I was committed to maintaining our marriage as it was, but times and experiences showed me that disappointment was always lurking around the corner. If I wasn't at work or doing activities with the children, I was watching TV, or on social media. Social media began to grow in popularity, and it was sometime during my mid-30s that I thought of My Marine while scrolling. I no longer resented or had bitterness towards him. I searched for him and found him. I attempted to be nosey and see what his life and marriage were like, but there wasn't much on his page. There were only sports pictures. I sent him a friend request. He accepted, but no messages followed. We were simply social media friends. I continued with my life and didn't think much of it afterwards.

As time passed, my primary focus continued to be on being a good mother and raising my children. For the benefit of keeping the family together and creating a stable home, the marriage continued. We didn't move as a team or as a partnership, but I became great at creating the "happily married" front to the outside world. At work, schools, events, church, we were happily married. There were times when we would have glimpses of happiness if it involved the children. Otherwise, we weren't generally in the same spaces at the same times. Over the course of years, there were instances of random phone numbers of women, which caused me to remember when I was the woman who went through their husband's phone. I'm not proud of that.

My experience in finding what you're looking for led me to be a woman who didn't even go looking. If I felt like I needed to investigate something, the problem was already there. Doubt, mistrust, and lack of transparency created an undercurrent of resentment that built up over time. The level of betrayal and emotional turmoil caused by the trauma of seeing messages or pictures of your partner with another person is unbearable and should never be minimized. I stopped looking through his phone after the last time I suspected something going on. I recognized how much damage it did to me and how long it affected me. Don't get me wrong, if I suspected something or was uneasy, I would still confront him. I just decided that I wouldn't snoop or play detective through his phone anymore. Looking back, I see that was growth. I recognized that if you feel the need to snoop, you already have your answer. There is a problem.

With time I had become braver and stronger. I became a fighter who was no longer sitting in the corner of the ring. I had to stand up for myself when I needed to. I wanted to keep my family together, but there were too many behaviors that I looked over in order to keep us together. The children were my primary motivation. There is something to be said about how damaging history can be to a relationship. There is also no way to determine how impactful the loss of trust can be. Our marriage should have grown in strength over the years, but in our case, it grew increasingly worse. Between our individual personal traumas, distrust, alcoholism, and the regular impacts of raising children and careers, it is amazing that we were able to keep our family together for the years that we had.

The Family Friend

During this period of our marriage my husband was laid off from work at the beginning of summer and didn't gain any additional employment for a while. He received a severance check and stated he would look for work at the end of summer. This caused stress to run high. We were going about our day-to-day lives as normal, and as I've mentioned before, throughout the marriage I was the CEO of our lives. I would create plans, and activities so we could have memorable family moments. It was important to me that the children have memorable family experiences that our lifestyle could afford them. This included vacations, trips, and sports that they were able to have varied exposure to what was available to them.

On this one particular weekend after a full Saturday of kayaking at the National Harbor, we returned home and were working on putting a new color of paint on the hallway walls. That was the weekend family project both Saturday and Sunday. Unfortunately, this was minus My Husbands participation. He often didn't care to be involved in any household upkeep or maintenance of the home. On Sunday evening my oldest daughter invited a friend (they were both juniors in college, ages 20 and 21) over to spend the night. This friend had been over to our house many times over the years. She also had attended some of our family trips since middle school days. There was a level of familiarity and comfort with her being around and in the home. Having our daughter's friend over had never been an issue in the past, because they had been best friends for years. I have always viewed her as a bonus daughter, and recently her mother had become a great new friend to me.

The friend helped paint as we worked in the hallway that evening. As far as I was concerned, having the Family Friend over had never been a concern. Yet, what was about to happen still perplexes me. There are still things I don't understand or possibly know about this situation. And, of all of the things that had happened in our marriage up to this point, I would never have expected this. It shook my marriage to the core because it revealed my ex-husband's lack of integrity, morals, and total disrespect for me as his wife, his family, the Family Friend, and her family.

On Monday morning the week started off with as much normalcy as possible. I took my youngest daughter to summer camp and went on to work. My oldest daughter went to work for a shift, which left her friend and my husband at home alone. I wasn't aware that she was left there alone with him until after the fact. I did question why the Family Friend chose to stay and not go home when my daughter went in to work. A few hours into my workday meeting I got a phone call on my cellphone. At that time, I was visiting a worksite and was unable able to answer the call right away. It was from the Mom of my daughter's friend, but for forty-five minutes to an hour I was unable to answer calls. I didn't think much of it and turned my ringer off until I was able to get back to my car. By the time I got to my car, I had several missed calls from the Family Friend's Mom. I called her back, and she answered immediately. What she told me over the phone emotionally shook me.

The mom was upset and said how that morning she saw her daughter through the window driving quickly down the street and then quickly rushing into their home. When her daughter came into the house she was visibly upset. She had to repeatedly ask her what was wrong. She went on to say that her daughter reluctantly explained what had happened that morning between her and my husband. As soon as she heard everything, she called me. The daughter explained that my husband and her talked about drinking together, so he went and bought liquor for them both and brought it back to the house. They shared some drinks and after a few too many there was some thigh rubbing and a kiss between them.

Immediately, after getting off the phone with her, I tried calling my husband. He wasn't answering the phone. After several calls he finally answered, and I could tell that he was intoxicated. When I arrived home, I tried to get information out of him, but it was pretty much the same thing that I was told by the Mom. It was a wild time because his story was less detailed than the Mom's. It was a very stressful evening. It remained like that for the next several weeks. We had a 10-year-old in the house who needed to be protected from whatever chaos that was happening in the home around her.

I was alone in this turmoil. I found it difficult to even speak to one of my best friends about what was happening in my life. Despite it not being my actions but My Husband's, it was embarrassing. It was embarrassing to me that the man I was married to had it in him to behave this way. I questioned myself as to how I could have been so ignorant to have married a man that was capable to do something like that. I was affected. My oldest daughter was affected, and I was married to that.

Eventually my oldest daughter spoke to me about it and relayed the incident as she was given it directly from her friend. It was described to me that once my husband

and the family friend were left alone, the two of them discussed getting drinks. My Husband went to the store that morning and bought them alcohol to share. I have no idea how much he bought, how much they drank, if they both drank or if only one of them had a drink. However, it was detailed to me that the family friend was sitting in our bedroom on the bed with him. My Husband rubbed on her thigh and proceeded to kiss her. I have no idea if the kiss was initially welcomed or was it rejected. I only know what the Family Friends Mom and what my oldest daughter said to me. I felt My Husband was not a reliable source of truth.

As you can imagine this affected the marriage, my daughter's friendship, and completely severed the fairly new friendship I had been building with the Family Friend's mom. At one point they had regarded us as bonus parents to their daughter. I felt the same way. We had known them since the girls were middle school age. I believe my Husband and the Family Friend's Father met and had a man-to-man conversation, but I'm not absolutely sure if it happened or not. During this time, I was in so much emotional turmoil, I was just trying to function as normal. Work, volunteering, being a mother and just trying to live. Emotionally I was all over the place. This was another level of the humiliation and embarrassment that alcoholism attributed to. In some ways this was one of the incidents that showed how I could no longer contain or control the impact of his alcoholism. I could no longer have the kids do things in their rooms or shut their doors after bedtime. One daughter was ten and the other twenty in college. The problem of alcoholism affecting the family was getting bigger and bigger. The problem was getting so big, it was spilling into every part of our lives.

Amazingly, following the event, my daughter and her friend were able to maintain their friendship. Not surprisingly, they are not as close as they once were, but they are friends. I have never spoken with her mom again. That was a real loss for me, because she was one of the few people in Maryland, I had made friends with. I eventually confided in a long-time friend a few states away, and she was extremely supportive. The ability to have a friendship with someone you trust is of immeasurable value.

It took a long time for me to move forward in the marriage after this situation. Despite staying in the marriage, it did continue to deteriorate. Our youngest daughter was still very young, and I wanted her to have the benefit of having both of her parents in the home to raise her. I would say that we were roommates, but we weren't. We functioned under the same roof. Although we had been in marital counseling prior to this incident, I was now completely done with marital counseling, and I didn't care that he wanted to return. I had no willingness to attend. I had no desire to fix what was broken. If we were supposedly actively working on our relationship and didn't suppress this type of betrayal, the relationship was likely too far gone. I was done with trying to fix everything. I slept in the bedroom and my husband slept in the family room on the couch. Life would be like this sporadically for the next few years. I don't believe I have ever truly forgiven him for this. Marriage is just paper without trust. I knew I was in the marriage for the benefit of the family and not for myself.

Life was difficult for me during this time. I was unhappy and alone without any support system. I found joy only in being a mother and doing volunteer work. I was very isolated in the life that I had chosen for myself. The outside world likely saw smiles, but internally I was often drained and annoyed at what my home life was like. The saying of "I don't look like what I've been through" is valid. There are likely people who probably never suspected the sadness or turmoil that I was living through day to day.

TL Phillips

Living on Autopilot

It would be like this for the next few years. Even after My Husband regained full-time employment our relationship never returned to a resemblance of what it was in our first few years of marriage. The years continued to pass, and the children continued to grow older as did we. What we held between us was a marriage on paper. A marriage that was a distant, limited communication, going-through-the-motions style relationship. We still attended events as a family or as a couple, if necessary, for family reunions, fraternity functions, and birthday parties. We had smiles plastered on our faces, but the love was lost in all of the pain, resentment, and disappointment. By this time, I would say our common interest together was only in being married. I wasn't the person for him, and he wasn't the person for me.

When I lost my mother in 2017 following months of her dealing with Bladder Cancer and therapy, something changed within me. It is fair to say my grief was very heavy. As a result, I was merely functioning and continuing in my responsibilities. There were glimmers of joy, but I was merely functioning within my grief. My tolerance and ability to "go with the flow" went away when the heaviness of the grief began to impact me. The responsibility of handling the grief of her death and tying up her estate was a heavy weight. I was emotionally struggling to function in my day-to-day life. By 2018, I was on autopilot, working, caring, and looking out for my children while maintaining the façade of efficiency while continuing my volunteer work. The relationship with my husband was over emotionally and physically. We were married in name, space and in appearances to the world. Nothing more. This level of marriage was completely fine with me. The stability of the children was the highest priority to me.

With the loss of my Mother, I came to recognize that living like this in a marriage was the furthest thing from what she wanted for me or what I wanted for myself. I no longer wanted or was willing to be married like this. I did not want this lifestyle to be the image of what my daughters would think of love. I wanted to be a better example of what a woman was. I recognized remaining in a marriage in which I wasn't loved, respected, or cared for wasn't a positive example at all. That idea of womanliness and marriage wasn't the life I was living, and I realized it needed to stop.

Around this time, My Husband had lost his job and was laid off again. He was in a contract position so there wasn't a severance package, just unemployment insurance. As you can imagine, unemployment checks barely covered his personal bills. No matter what amount it was, My Husband was no longer contributing anything financial to the household. He was able to afford his alcohol and cigarette habits. A few months after losing his job, it was apparent to me that I needed to make more money to make ends meet. I had enough to cover all bills and private school tuition, but I was falling short in affording groceries once the household bills were paid. Our youngest child was in her sophomore year in a private school, and I felt pulling her out because of her parent's money problems wasn't fair to her. So, in order to maintain and make everything continue to happen, I cut back and reduced as many expenses as possible. I even began working a part-time position at FedEx loading trailers from 5:30-10:30 pm.

This was what my life had become. Working two jobs, one of which was physical labor despite holding an advanced degree. To say that there was a level of resentment towards my husband during this time would be an understatement. I had two jobs, and he didn't have one. I was working hard without any relief or support.

When I suggested he work for Uber, he told me he tried but that it wasn't for him. My husband wasn't cleaning the house, making meals, or working, but he still managed to smoke and get drunk.

I would come in from working the second job, usually close to 11 pm and most times the house would be quiet from everyone sleeping, or he would be up watching tv. There was no love or grace for me found at home. Either way, no one would take the opportunity to fix a meal for me or even slap a sandwich together. All the while, I am working this job so that I can purchase groceries every week and sustain the family's lifestyle. I was doing everything I could, but I had a spouse who had no interest in helping or being supportive. This was my life.

To me, it was even more apparent that the only interest My Husband had in me was being a provider. He did not care about me or my well-being. The only love that I had was from my children. I was in this struggle alone. During this period, I was still grieving the loss of my mother, so my internal sadness was at an all-time high and there was no relief in sight. I was a shell of my former self.

That summer I suggested my husband apply for a teaching position. I wanted him to attend a teacher hiring event because he had a degree. I was hoping he would get hired. He attended. Thankfully, he was hired by the county school system and began working that fall.

My life still consisted of work, work, work. There was our youngest daughter's cheer game schedule, volunteering for Girl Scouts, my part-time job, serving as the parent board vice president, and other outside activities. I continued the part-time position after My Husband began working, because he stated he would need a few months to recover financially from being unemployed before he would be able to start paying half of the household bills. When I wasn't out busy doing those things, I sat in the chair and watched TV. Life in the house was very quiet. Everyone gravitated to their own solitude. If it didn't involve being in the kitchen or laundry, I remained in the sitting room. Within the house I only had conversations with my children.

TL Phillips

Covid-19 Pandemic

By the time the Covid-19 pandemic shut down began across the country, my husband and I hadn't been sexually active for almost two years. Kissing had ceased years ago due to his constant smoking. Even though many years have passed, I still find cigarette smoking unattractive. My interest or desire for him was completely and absolutely gone. I knew I was done with any type or any level of relationship outside of being the family. My last day in the work office was on March 30, 2020, and I quit the part-time job at FedEx. My adult daughter and I were working from home, and my youngest daughter was doing her high school classes from home.

My husband on the other hand did not start working from home right away. The school system was large, and the logistics of the classroom had not happened, making his days open and free. Yet, my husband was leaving the house and returning home five to six hours later. We only spoke to each other when absolutely necessary. So even though he was "disappearing" during the day, I didn't have much to say, while always paying attention to what was happening.

This was a scary time for the entire country as a whole and it was scary for me as an individual and parent. The news media was non-stop about the pandemic. Most people were probably watching the news non-stop. I don't think anything has gripped the nation like this since the 9/11 attacks. My fear and anxiety escalated with seeing the death toll quickly rising across the US. As a parent, we often strive to protect our children and from my perspective, My Husband wasn't protecting them or me by being "out" daily doing whatever it was that he was doing. He wasn't out being an essential worker because teaching was not essential "out of the house" work. We had no knowledge of where he was, what he was doing, or if he was being exposed to the virus that was killing people.

It didn't take long before these disappearances began to make me angry and scared for the safety of all of us in the house. We had no idea what he was doing outside or if he was possibly getting exposed to and contracting Covid. If he was getting exposed, he was bringing it back to the house and risking everyone's life without any concern or hesitation. I thought if he wouldn't protect this family I would have to. In the midst of my frustration, I decided to contact a family member asking if we could come and stay there. I assured him that we would be careful and cautious and that we would not be a disruption to his life.

The next morning My Husband left the house again, and I made the decision to leave. I told my children to pack a bag and that we were leaving and going out of town. I told the children it was an effort to keep everyone safe. I called My Husband several times with no answer. There was no response to my text messages either. This wasn't unusual behavior for us. He hadn't responded to calls or text messages from me in a timely fashion in years. He responded whenever he felt like it. After not receiving any calls back, I began asking my children to call him. Both of them attempted to reach him from their cellphones, but didn't get a response either. My oldest daughter advised me that she wasn't going to travel with me because she didn't want to leave him by himself. Since she was an adult, I knew I couldn't make her come with me or try to convince her to leave. I was disappointed that she wouldn't come with me and let me protect her from Covid-19.

My other child was upset that I was making her leave, but she wasn't grown so I had to decide, for her protection. I waited until two thirty that afternoon for My Husband's return. That was just enough time to get us to our destination before it was dark out. With feelings of fear, uneasiness, anxiety, and stress we packed the car and drove to Hampton.

Back In Hampton

As most people can recall, the Covid-19 pandemic was a highly stressful time for most. I thankfully was able to work 100% remotely and my high school daughter was able to resume classes remotely as well. This was a blessing, because there were so many people who were completely out of work and didn't have income for their basic human needs.

I felt the relief of not dealing with alcoholism and smoke in the house or around me in just a few days. Even with the gloom and doom of Covid-19 with its rising death toll, it was as though a cloud was lifted in the sky and weights were removed from my shoulders. Although returning to Hampton limited me to protecting only one child, I quickly realized by making this choice I removed her from the dysfunction of seeing and experiencing alcoholism firsthand in her daily life. She may never be able to understand or comprehend the need for me to bring her to Hampton, but it was a positive thing. I don't regret that choice.

My daughter still doesn't understand why I did what I did. I do think she appreciated or saw the reason behind it. It definitely wasn't to hurt her or her dad. It was always about her safety as well as my own. My husband, due to his alcoholism, always, always, always put his needs first and let the chips fall where they may. That behavior was selfish, but I do recognize alcoholism as a disease, and no one wants a disease. This decision to return to Hampton squarely placed the needs of us ahead of My Husband's selfishness and alcoholism, even though my oldest daughter did not come with us.

At some point during the 16 years of marriage, I had evolved into less of a wife and more of a mother to My Husband. He maneuvered and functioned like a boy trapped in a man's body. Instead of two children in the home, I had three for years, and it was a weight too heavy to bear. As a parent, it is often necessary to think three steps down the line in case something goes wrong for your children. As a married person, one of the benefits is that there are two people in alignment thinking for the benefit of the children as well as for the household as a whole, providing and protecting the family. After living through a marriage of turmoil and disappointments, the benefits or gains of being married were almost always about what was best for my children. Me and my happiness were secondary. It had always been that way. I had been handling and running the family while treating myself as less important. I was now at a place where it was increasingly difficult to put myself on the back burner.

I definitely wish I had done things differently in my marriage. I had attempted to be supportive and keep our family together through alcoholism. Alcoholism created a life of stress and uncertainty, which included two attempts at in-treatment rehab, betrayals, and disrespect. Not long after arriving in Hampton, I realized that I no longer had the willingness to continue with that life. I no longer felt that I had the ability or strength to put everyone else's needs or desires above my own. I was functioning and attempting to keep a marriage together even though there was no emotional, financial, or mental security for me. I provided these things for others. I recognize that my needs matter too, even if there was no one around who believed it. My proverbial cup was close to empty, and no one was going to fill it up but me.

It had become abundantly clear that I was never a priority for anyone. I had placed myself or allowed myself to be secondary behind keeping our family together and it still had been dysfunctional. There was no happiness for any of us in the family because of the dysfunction. I had sacrificed myself for our family unit, but the family unit was hurting each of us more by remaining together than letting it go. Having lost my mother a few years back, it was clear to me that there was no one who was walking this earth that I was a priority for. I came to the realization that I mattered to no one in a significant way outside of being a parent. I had to become a priority for myself.

The pandemic, working from home, and currently away from my primary stressor, I was able to sit and think about my life. I realized that at some point during the marriage and raising the children, I had completely lost myself. I had dimmed my own light and continuously contorted myself into a false image, trying to maintain a family and be an honorable wife who wasn't respected. I recognized I was in a relationship where I received no love, care, or intimacy and I wanted more for myself. I wanted love for my life again. I no longer had the patience or desire to continue in the marriage. I no longer wanted to be married for the sake of being married. Being in Hampton working remotely due to Covid gave me the opportunity to think without the distractions.

The stress of alcoholism, the need to cover and distract from a possible episode breaking out when my husband came into the home drunk was easing. And I came to recognize that in choosing to remain married, I would never be happy. So much damage had already been done and neither of us would ever be able to lower the walls to let each other in at this point. I had to acknowledge that the marriage was done. It had just been on life support. It was time to pull the plug. When I came to the realization that I would rather get divorced and possibly be single for the rest of my life was better than remaining in a loveless marriage, my decision was made. During this time, I received one call from my future ex-husband in which he told me to come home. I asked one simple question, "Why?" His response was, "because I said so." I laughed. That conversation was over. That was the one and only conversation (if you can call it that) about reconciliation that we had.

Getting divorced in my late forties would be scary, but the risk was clear to me. Either stay in the relationship that I knew was over or step out on faith to be happy and safe alone. If love is meant for me, it will come for me. I had finally made the decision that I couldn't do it anymore and began taking steps towards divorce.

I have never regretted making that choice. The only thing I regret is not having done it sooner. Had I made the choice sooner, several of the major incidents of the marriage would never have happened. There would have been less damage and trauma to have healed from for me and others. From Hampton I contacted my attorney and began the process of a formal separation and divorce. It began within a matter of days. Separation and divorce agreements were made over the next few months with little resistance from my Future Ex-husband.

The Return to Maryland

Several months into the summer, our youngest daughter's private school announced the planning of a hybrid schedule for the upcoming school year. I began speaking with my Future Ex-husband about leaving Hampton and returning to Maryland so our daughter could attend classes as scheduled. The divorce was becoming a reality, and my Future Ex-husband and I discussed and agreed that in order for us to return to the local area, he would need to move out of the house. With that assurance, I made the plan to return to Maryland.

When we arrived back in Maryland that August, my Future Ex-husband was not only not packed or moved out, but he was also intoxicated. Thirty minutes into our arrival he had punched and broke a window. and refused to leave the house as agreed and then he laid out as though he had passed out. The girls were happy about the return to Maryland, but I wasn't. My stress and anxiety quickly returned. I now had a dilemma to face. If we returned to Hampton, my daughter wouldn't be able to continue with her junior year at the Maryland school since it would no longer be 100% remote. If I left her there without me, it would be a risk if her Father wasn't able to take care of her and ensure she attended classes for the hybrid school schedule. I didn't know what to do.

Eventually I made the decision to stick it out and stay in the house even with him being there. I was sick of bending for his benefit. With my Future Ex-husband pulling this "I refuse to leave" stunt, I had nothing else to say if it wasn't about our daughter or the divorce. I stayed in the owner's bedroom, and he slept on the couch in the family room. Over the next few months, the drunkenness continued around us. There were incidents that continued to happen that made it extremely difficult to function within these circumstances. It was difficult for me and difficult for the children. If he wasn't in the house, the girls and I quarantined ourselves in our bedrooms and kept the doors shut most of the time.

At this point during the Covid-19 pandemic, I was still working 100% remotely and was still expecting to get through this divorce with as little tension as possible. I was planning to move back to Hampton as soon as the school year ended. With everything that was happening, the school year couldn't end fast enough. This marriage chapter of my life needed to end.

Death and Disease

As with many people during this time, I used social media more consistently than I had ever had before with all of the years of having it. One evening as I was randomly scrolling through my feed, I saw posts with My Marine tagged to it. By now we had been social media friends for close to ten years. I honestly don't ever recall seeing any posts from him over the years, but all of a sudden, his name was tagged in a bunch of posts. I took the time to go through the pictures of the post just looking for his face. There were several pictures with groups of people, and I recognized a few faces. He wasn't there. The people in the photos were his family, and they were together in fellowship over the death of a patriarch of the family. His grandfather.

I quickly remembered how much his grandfather meant to him, and how he loved and admired him. I could only imagine the pain and heartbreak he must have been feeling. This would have been a huge loss for him. A gut-wrenching loss. I could empathize with what he might have been feeling because it was a feeling I knew so well with the passing of my mom. A part of me felt his loss so much so that although I was hesitant and nervous about reaching out. I did. After over 10 years of being "friends" on social media, I reached out for the first time. I didn't think that it would be weird. Neither of us should be bitter nor upset about the past. But because of how we ended, there was no way to know how it would be received. I had grown to understand how much My Marine meant to me years ago. I understood I had love for him. I also knew I was just a blip on the timeline of his life. Just a memory of a young love.

I didn't reach out to him immediately since my circumstances were weird. It would be hard to explain how I was married but living in Maryland and getting a divorce while sharing a home with my soon-to-be ex-husband. So even though I hadn't seen or spoken to My Marine in thirty years, I nervously took a moment to send my condolences to him via messenger and held my breath. Maybe he would respond. Maybe he wouldn't, but I wished him the best. To my surprise, he responded thanking me for the sentiment. My Marine not only thanked me, but there was also some general conversation between us. In an ending message, he also sent me his phone number and said to "break the glass." The interaction in the messages was nice and sweet. All animosity between us seemed to be long gone.

Thirty years had passed. I was now curious about him, and I wanted to know what his life had become. One evening when I was out picking up my dog from the groomer, I called the number from my car. I knew that voice! He sounded the same. To say that hearing his voice brought me joy and nervousness would be an understatement. My heart raced with excitement just like it had done years before. I knew even then I had never stopped loving him. I had just moved on. Good, bad, or indifferent, I had moved on and had a full life without him. That evening's call brought My Marine back into my world. Slowly and consistently, we shared what our lives had been without each other. What we had accomplished and done differently since the last time we were connected.

We talked for about 30-40 minutes on that first call. He had just gotten home from work. When we first started communicating with each other, we were very friendly and casual. It wasn't every day. The birthday and holiday greetings were friendly and casual. Once the new year rang in things began to gain speed up. We started texting back and forth constantly every day. Hundreds of texts between the two of us. Calls and Facetime were fewer because of the six-hour time difference. In many ways, him being in Hawaii and me being in Maryland was good for us. It was safe. We were able to get to know each other again without going too quickly.

When I looked back over our previous life together, we moved quickly, hot, and heavy mostly due to our age and immaturity led only with our hearts. This was different. We were older. We could utilize our head and hearts if that's what we both chose to do. I enjoyed getting to know him again. Communicating with him started to become the highlight of my days. My Marine told me that over the years he'd always talked about me. He said he would tell his friends about me, and they would say to him that he was still in love with me. He told me that he had always believed we would reconnect again and rewrite our story. The first few months he was very adamant in convincing me that he had always loved me. This was something that came up often between conversations. I hadn't believed that he could have married so quickly if he had actually loved me back then. I needed reassurance. I didn't know if I believed him even though I really had wanted to. I wasn't sure if I could trust him with my heart again.

He told me all about what his life had been like after we split. About his marriage. About his changes in temperament and how he saw the world now. He explained how he had been choosing to work on himself for the last few years. As far as I believed, he showed me his soul. My Marine told me the good, the bad, and the ugly of who he was over the years that brought him to be the man who I was talking to now. I was promised that he would never hurt me again and if I gave him this chance, he would always do his part. Due to the time difference, I would text him at his wake-up time and try to stay up late to text him soon after he got off of work at 2:30 pm Hawaii time.

On one particular night during our conversation, he texted me that he loved me. I hadn't expected it, and it had caught me off guard. Our conversations were great. We were getting to know each other again and building our friendship. It was still fairly early in our reconnection. When I saw the text, I didn't know what to do. I literally sat up in the bed, because seeing those words on the screen scared me. I looked at it and hesitated because it knocked me off guard. I wasn't expecting this from him. Not this soon. It had only been a few months of us really getting to know each other again. Tears slid down my face. Five thousand miles away and My Marine still affected me. Him expressing himself like this scared me because he had hurt me so badly years before. I didn't know if I could trust him again. I knew he was being vulnerable with me, but was I safe with him? I didn't even know how to respond to those words. I didn't know if he was safe for me to trust again.

Remember I told you about My Marine telling me he loved me? All of this is happening simultaneously with the heavy news surrounding my Future Ex-husband. I no longer have the texts to reference, so I am not sure if I responded saying thank you or what I'm not sure. What I do know is that me not responding, "I love you" right away was not because I didn't love him, it was because of fear. Thirty years ago, I had decided to move on and let our relationship go because I could no longer trust him and believe in him. Our new connection was still very fresh, and my guard was still up, but his vulnerability in that moment did affect me. My guard quickly came down after that night.

Even though he was being so open and so straight forward, I was scared he was going to hurt me again if I opened up to him. Eventually, I did get to the point of telling him how much I loved him. I shared with him how when we split up it wasn't that I stopped loving him. One thing that moment told me was that our love was mutual. He loved me. He had never stopped loving me. I was loved by him just as deeply as I had always loved him. I had never stopped loving him. I do know that the way I responded was not how he wanted me to, and he would bring it up months later. During that conversation, he mentioned that he had laid all of his feelings out there and I didn't tell him I loved him too. That had hurt him, and I didn't mean to, but I had. Me trying to protect myself from a hurt that I never wanted to feel again actually hurt him in the process.

Later in that month, my oldest daughter came to me visibly upset. It was revealed to me that my Future Ex-husband had confided in her that he had been diagnosed with Cancer. She stated she felt helpless and didn't know what to do. Being that I had lost my Mother to a form of cancer, this was very heavy information. First-hand experience of losing someone from cancer makes hearing this type of news more impactful. Then something changed. Something clicked in my mind. As my daughter continued talking, she mentioned that she was told not to tell me. I thought to myself that it was strange for him to tell her that specifically.

Internally I thought and questioned why he would put this type of burden on her. So, I began asking questions such as "did he tell your brother too?" He hadn't. My brain began running a mile a minute. "Why would he tell her and not to tell me something that important? Why wouldn't he tell his only son? Why would he put this burden on her? Why would he give her this burden at her age, instead of one of his friends?" All of these questions sped through my mind. I became upset and I also became suspicious. I suspected that either he shared this to garner sympathy from her or that he was simply lying.

Within the hour, I was reaching out to my stepson, to advise him of the information that had been shared by his Father. While all of this was happening, their Father was laid out intoxicated on the couch. It was a daily norm at this point. If he was not working, he would be out in the streets and when he returned, he was laid out sleeping off his intoxication on the couch. After speaking with the two oldest children about my future ex-husband's cancer diagnosis, the more and more I suspected that he was lying about it to gain sympathy. I stated in the conversation with the adult kids that we would not be telling their youngest sibling of what was happening in case it was all a lie. After that discussion, I then contacted one of my future ex-husband's closest friends. Interestingly enough one of my ex-husband's best friends, is named Pat. I had never considered until then that people with the name of Pat seem to always be the couriers of bad news.

Due to the cancer "scare," I had reached out to Pat. In that conversation with him, he shared he had not been contacted or made aware of any news since he was told about me filing for a divorce. Pat shared a great deal of information about my husband and marriage that I hadn't expected as well. During this long conversation, he led by telling me that if I was considering not going through with the divorce that I should definitely go through with it. I was likely on the phone with him for over an hour's time if not longer. During that conversation, it was revealed that he had cheated on multiple occasions with different people. Pat revealed that one thing that really bothered him, but he never spoke about through the years, was the misunderstanding I had about him. I had come to him years prior about being a bad influence, taking my husband out drinking so much. He stated that it was my husband who always wanted to go out, not him. Pat stated that my future ex-husband had always had a problem with alcoholism and would borrow money just so that he could stay out and drink ever since he had known him. The next few hours solidified the image of what I thought of my Future Ex-husband. As a result, I have had no regrets on moving forward with my life and getting a divorce.

Side Note: Going forward, any man that I get involved with who has a friend named Pat will likely not remain in my life for good measure. That is a new life rule!

Over the next few days, I tried getting information about my Future Ex-husband's condition. I was unable to because I was not authorized. I continued to check in with our adult children about his status and even confronted him asking for any paperwork that was provided from the doctors about the type of cancer or what information was shared from the doctors. He had nothing to show me. No resources, pamphlets, or printouts. Nothing. I knew this was irregular for US medical office practices. In my experience, when my Mother was being treated for her cancer, there wasn't an appointment that did not produce paperwork, especially during those first few visits.

After repeatedly questioning my Future Ex-husband about what he should have gotten from the doctors eventually revealed that he had never been diagnosed with cancer. He had been assessed due to the cough he had and hadn't been able to shake. A test. He was tested for his cough, not diagnosed with cancer. Realistically I can understand his concern considering he had been a smoker, but it didn't justify the lie. He chose to burden our daughter with something that he knew was untrue to garner a level of sympathy from her. At this moment I had literally no sympathy for him and found myself being annoyed and disgusted by him.

Between the firsthand of the experience of our relationship and the confession from his closest friends, my emotions and feelings were so detached from him. Me getting a divorce was long overdue. I wished I had done it years earlier. It couldn't get finalized fast enough for me.

About two weeks later my stepson came to town to visit his dad. During this visit, he, my oldest daughter, and I went out to lunch in honor of my 50th birthday. Over this meal, we discussed the supposed cancer scare. They both behaved how I expected. They were generally very sympathetic about the situation despite having been lied to. My Future Ex-husband's behavior was in fact to get sympathy, and when it didn't play out, he wasn't being held accountable. They were always sympathetic with him. They gave the impression and behaved as though this lack of accountability or responsibility never bothered them. I knew I couldn't continue living and functioning under the same roof no matter what. It was time to face the fact that I would have to move out and let the house go into foreclosure if he wasn't willing to be financially responsible without my income. It was time to just cut my losses. I was weary of having to deal with the messes of my Future Ex-husband, but this was just too much. I had to get out of that house as soon as possible. I didn't want to wait until the end of the school year, which was three long months away.

Before the end of March, I received my signed final divorce decree. I was officially divorced. I had also reached out to a family member in Greensboro and a friend in Atlanta, asking if I could come stay with them. I wanted to start a new chapter in a new-to-me city but unfortunately neither of them said yes. Neither was able to help for their own personal reasons. I didn't like it, but I know very well that you seldom fully know what other people have going on behind their closed doors. My remaining option was to return back to my hometown of Hampton. I began looking for work there and began planning to move in June 2021, when my youngest daughter's junior high school year ended. I had a plan.

Reunited

About a month and a half later, late April 2021, My Marine came to the East Coast to see me and visit with his family. He flew to Maryland, and I was able to pick him up from the airport. It was the first time I had laid eyes on him in over 30 years. There was nothing but joy having him in my arms again! I visited him only a few times while he stayed at his friend's house and then we vacationed for a week in Williamsburg together. I had My Marine, and I was his Baby, once again. There was a sense of newness and excitement between us. It was the first time that I was able to see some of his behavior differences live and in effect. I was able to be clingy and "hug up" on him as long as he was able to sometimes have time by himself whenever he needed it. With the knowledge of us both being in love with each other, we were fine. I was the face on his lockscreen. That wasn't the only lock. He was locked in and so was I. We had a quiet, loving vacation together.

After putting him on his flight May 11th and getting back to our regular routines, upon his suggestion I began looking for work in Hawaii. As someone who never even considered going to Hawaii for even a vacation, I began considering it as a new chapter for our love story. I began applying for positions and progress happened fairly quickly. I probably applied for a dozen different positions. It was a surprise how quickly it all moved. Faster than I ever expected. I was called for one interview and received a tentative job offer within ten days. I had been praying so hard during this period. I was scared. This move would solidify "us" again. Our relationship would no longer be long distance. I was nervous. I was really, really scared.

Although My Marine said my daughter could come with me and live with him, she didn't want to go. Being that it was her upcoming senior year, I didn't want to force her. If I got a firm job offer. I would make the decision to step out on faith and move 5,000 miles to be with the love of my life. I was all in. This new chapter of my life meant I would have to leave my youngest baby and entrust her care with her older sister and her alcoholic Father. This required me to pray and pray hard. I had to believe and be serious about what I was willing to do for my personal happiness and to make our new relationship work. By the end of June, I received the final job offer. I knew this was God working on my behalf. I have never doubted that. Nothing and no one will ever convince me that it was not the Lord working on my behalf to make that transition so smooth! God has never failed me!

A few weeks prior to my arrival, My Marine began saying that he didn't want us to live together. Knowing that he didn't want to "live in sin" or do things like he had done before, I respected that. He wasn't sure if he was ready for this move. When he told me on the phone, he didn't want us to live together, it was scary. By this point, I had already accepted the position, and I knew I couldn't make this leap without him. So,

I asked if he would let me live with him for a few months in order to get settled and then I would find a place of my own. That is what we agreed upon. I did become a bit apprehensive about what his intention with me was and then he assured me, "Baby, it will be fine. I will do my part." So, I chose to trust him.

We were well on our way to being able to dance to "My First, My Last, My Everything" (Barry White) one day. I believed and trusted in him again and I believed in us. I had to trust him. Our relationship would not work if I didn't trust him. He had assured me that he would do his part for our relationship, and I have never doubted him.

I did recognize that coming to Hawaii would require understanding where he was emotionally. Although it was his idea that I come, the reality might have felt different now that it was actually happening, and the ball was rolling. Everything could not and would not be just how I wanted it to be but that is the reality of relationships. In general, it would require commitment, understanding, and sacrifice for us to have our happy ending this time. His openness about how his PTSD has affected him over the years required my patience and understanding to get to our happy ending. My Marine said he wanted us and that he wanted a title. He gave me assurances consistently before making this leap.

Hawaii

Coming to Hawaii was me choosing him. It was choosing a new life with the greatest love of my life. I intended for My Marine to be the first and last love I would ever have. He would be the last person I love, care for, kiss, and be intimate with for the rest of my life. We were each other's person, and this was our love story. He and I were going to have our happy ending this time. We were fortunate to have been given this second chance, and we weren't going to waste it. Our story had begun in Hampton, and we reconnected over 5,000 miles away from each other. Our love would continue to develop, heal, and grow in Hawaii, and we would retire back in Hampton after a few years. That was the plan. Two months later, during the last week of July 2021, I was on a flight moving to Hawaii to start a new life with My Marine.

When I arrived, I got my first surprise when he picked me up from the airport. In the car, I was told that I would need to get my own bedding to stay in my room. I was like, "what?" I was shocked. This hadn't come up before. We had never discussed having separate rooms. He said he needed his space in the bed because it was an air mattress.

So, on the way in from the airport we stopped at a big box store, and I bought an air mattress and bedding for my room, separate from his. When I arrived at the apartment, the boxes that I had shipped in advance were in the second bedroom and after I set up my bed, put away the boxes, and showered, I had my first night in Hawaii in the bed with My Marine. I did not sleep in my room. My Marine is very guarded. However, him allowing me to come to Hawaii was him putting me within his walls. Not outside of them. This was something that only I was able to do, and I was made aware of this fact by him.

I wasn't scheduled to begin my new position until the next week, so I hung out at the house those first few days waiting for him to return from work each day. Each night we would talk to each other for hours, watch tv, and enjoy each other's company. As we were talking while I got settled in, he told me that no one else could have ever come to Hawaii. Only me. I was like, "really?" and he said yes. He mentioned other women he used to talk to had asked to visit when he had first moved, and the answer had always been no. Only me. My Marine would remind me, only "My Baby" could have come here. He stated that I was the closest person to him. That meant a great deal to me and revealed to me how special he saw me for his life.

The next day he told me how much I tossed and turned when I first fell asleep. We laughed about it. Knowing that it was an indicator of my stress and anxiety, we knew I would get more settled. This was real life, and we were living it. That was the beginning of our life together again.

My Marine was my King and without a doubt I knew he would die for me. He even told me so. There was nothing he would not do for me, and I believed him. I was his Queen, and I never doubted that either. The reality is that there were various dynamics of a King and Queen. When My Marine came back into my life, I became his Queen again; however, I wasn't as strong as I had once been. Life had battered me a bit. So, this time, it was necessary for my King to provide and protect me in a way that I had never experienced before. In a way that I had never needed him before. There is a saying, "I am a movement by myself, but a force when we are together." That is what I believed My Marine, and I were together. I felt the strength of his presence which allowed me to regain my own strength by his side.

When I arrived in Hawaii, it was necessary that he was able to financially cover and provide for me. I was financially struggling due to my recent divorce, despite having a good paying job. For several months after arriving, I was still paying half of the mortgage back on the east coast. When I shared this information with My Marine, he recommended I stop paying it because it was affecting me financially. I advised my Ex-husband, and I stopped covering half of the mortgage. Over time, I was able to recover economically and contribute easily to the Hawaii household.

Over the next few months of me arriving on the island, on various occasions I was told that he was not ready for a relationship. I didn't agree with his thinking, but I wanted to understand his needs. PTSD manifests differently in different people and based upon the love that I knew he had for me, I had to be understanding of his feelings, patient, and be sure to not minimize them. My Marine was different from who he was years ago in our young adulthood. He needed a great deal of solitude and quiet. More than I have ever seen in any adult. He was a different man. Even with these changes, I was told that I was the closest person to him and that he would never hurt me again. I believed him and that his intent was only for our good in the long run. I never doubted him, and I trusted him my entire life. There is no way I would have moved to Hawaii, if I hadn't believed we both wanted us.

To love, respect, and be loyal to each other to rewrite our love story.

Over the next few months, we began to learn each other again. One of the best memories I have from that first place in Pearl City, Hawaii, is him peaking his head into the bathroom and giving me a morning kiss on his way to work. It was just a sweet gesture, reminiscent of our early life together. Life was simple, quiet, and peaceful. Our new life together was easy, and comfortable. To love someone who had changed so much in the span of 30 years was challenging at times for both of us. The person I once knew was difficult and stubborn but could also be extremely loving and caring. Those traits were still there.

Before coming to Hawaii, he had told me that he had only driven around the island a few times. The times that he did drive were primarily to work, home, the grocery store, and car wash. He wasn't being social. He came up with a plan to heal himself and prepare for retirement. That is what he was doing. Labeling him as a recluse could be a step too far, but maybe that is exactly who he was. For the year and a half that we were under the same roof he had been that way. As a couple, we drove around the island only once together. Outside of that, he pretty much kept to his basic routine. I was the only one who would go out and do things on the island at nights or weekends.

He and I never got into shouting matches. Not once did I ever hear him yell or change his temperament in front of me. My Marine's anger issues seemed to definitely be in check. He was still very stubborn, but he was able to talk to me -- which was excellent for me because I didn't want a toxic type of life. I no longer wanted to be or was willing to deal with situations that would be so upsetting to me that screaming even seemed like an option. So, I absolutely loved that being upset or triggered wouldn't lead either of us to screaming and hollering. Our home wasn't a high anxiety environment. We had peace. Our life together was easy. Some of the best times we had were our ease and comfort talking, cuddling, watching tv, or sitting in complete silence. We had safety in our home. We would disagree, but it never escalated into an argument.

As we had originally agreed, I began looking for a place of my own after a few months. It wasn't what I wanted, but My Marine had made it clear he didn't want us to live together. He had said to me "I told you not to come. We would have been fine if you had stayed in Maryland." I don't know why he still wanted to do this. We had peace in our home, and we were happy, but I knew that just like 30 years prior, My Marine only does what he wants to do. People can influence him, but he will make a decision and stand ten toes down on it even if it turns out to be a bad one. He makes his own choices. If he was more comfortable with us not living together, I would be willing to try. So, this was always confusing for me because it was only his idea that I even came to Hawaii. However, we agreed on me getting my own place, and if that is what he needed for our relationship to work, I was fine with it. I began visiting various apartments around the island.

One evening in October after coming in from taking a tour of an apartment, he called me up from his room. When I came upstairs, he told me that he wanted us to stay together. I asked him if he was sure, and he said that he was. So that is what we did. I stopped looking for my own place because he wanted to continue our life together. About a month or so later, he was told we would have to move due to a real estate sale. While he was away visiting his family for Thanksgiving, I found a new place for us, about two streets over in the same complex we were currently living in. He gave his okay over the phone based on the photos and when he returned, we visited the new place in person.

In retrospect, I can only guess that he was having conversations about us to friends and family, minimizing what I was to him and building a cohort against me. I already knew that. Although some of his family seemed happy that I was back in his life, I had already gotten the feeling that one of his cousins wasn't particularly pleased. This can be expected sometimes from family and friends. From their perspective, some of them likely knew how bad our breakup was 30 years ago. Although time had passed, they may still have held a grudge against me for hurting him.

In December 2021, we moved into another townhouse. This is now our fourth place. We continued to keep our bedrooms separate and our relationship situationship continued. We were still loving, talking, and being each other's partner. As time went on, the title thing was something that I began having an issue with because it didn't make any sense to me. The dilemma for me was that I just didn't like not having an "official" title, but I really didn't want to pressure him either. But going with the flow was creating an internal issue for me. On the one hand I wasn't concerned about it because we were definitely together living our lives and because he had established the significance of who I was in his life. I did think he was getting better and becoming warmer over time, but I never wanted to push, overwhelm, or smother him. Attempting to be sensitive to his needs took effort. I didn't always do well, but I believe in most situations I was considerate. The entire time, I never saw his anger again from when we were young. He handled it differently, and he was never disrespectful to me -- especially those first few months we were back together. I cautiously looked for glimpses of his anger but never saw it.

I know there was no one else but me in his life. At no time since he had come back into my life had he ever given me a reason to doubt him. There was never a situation in which I felt that he was sneaking seeing someone or calling/texting anyone on an intimate level. Nothing like that. He would answer a phone call in front of me, hand me his phone, if need be, and keep it faced up if I were sitting next to it. There was never a scenario or behavior that made me question if I was his one and only. He knew why I was there, and I knew why I was there. The most important part of this life was that we were loving each other on our second chance.

One day when we were just laying around in his room watching TV on the bed, I started the conversation about him not wanting a title. I stated to him that I understood that he didn't want to do the title thing but that I needed to know was he committed to me. It was a statement more than a question that I needed an answer to. I was always sensitive to not want to push him, pressure or make him feel cornered so I said it as plain and openly as I could. This was an uncomfortable conversation for me, but I had to know if he was or wasn't still in this with me. If he was committed to me, I didn't need an official title right then. A commitment is a relationship. I knew it and he knew it. I could work with him and meet him where he was. I loved him and we were worth the sacrifice and patience. So, I asked him, "are you committed to me?" and without any hesitation his answer was "yes, you know I am." So, I continued to trust him.

The temperament that My Marine had was like a special need. It was a part of his unseen disability, and I gave him the time and space he needed and required. During the entire time we were under the same roof, I had someone who was still telling me he loved me. He was always consistent in how much he loved me. When he was out of town to visit family, he always told me he missed me. I believed him. I always believed him. I trusted him with my life. I never doubted his love for me.

For the next several months we were happy. Our home was peaceful, loving, nice, and lemon-scented clean. We were happy. We were both doing well at work, still learning, and enjoying each other again. I returned to the east coast for three weeks for my daughter's prom and graduation. During that time, we still talked daily. For convenience, I stayed in the house that I used to share with my ex-husband and family. I was aware of the jealous streak that My Marine had, so it was important to me to be sure to keep our communication open and transparent. I never wanted him to doubt me, especially in situations involving another man.

This high lasted about another six or seven months in the new place and then things changed drastically. I can recall our first spat in July. He got up from his bed and approached me as I stood in the doorway of his room and slowly closed the door in my face. This upset me. I was triggered, because I saw it as so disrespectful to shut a door in someone's face. I believe this was the first time I had become angry with him in the whole time I had been in Hawaii. Don't get me wrong, it wasn't a slam or aggressive in any manner, but it was definitely a closed door in my face. I was standing in the doorway of his room as we were going back and forth debating about a subject that I cannot even recall. We probably were going back and forth 15 minutes before he shut the door in my face. I wasn't irritated. I was angry. I was mad. I left out of the house and sent a text to him from the car stating that since he hadn't signed the new lease he had as much right to be in the house as the plants and he could move out.

I'm sure that wasn't received in any other way than with the pettiness it was intended. Needless to say, that text didn't go over well with him considering I had left him thirty years prior. It was an ultimatum of if you don't like it, then leave. As soon as I sent it, I knew I was wrong. When I came back a few hours later, I went into my room, and he was in his. We didn't speak for the remainder of the evening even though I knew I was wrong and should have apologized quickly. There was no way we could have a good relationship if either of us ever felt like their security was threatened. We were both being stubborn. The next day I went to him, and I apologized because I knew I was wrong to go there. I had lost my temper, but he viewed it as me being too sensitive or triggered. For several weeks, My Marine had little to say to me. We had our first big disagreement, and we weren't smoothing it out. He had begun to shut down. Over six months later My Marine told me that he had lost trust in me due to this disagreement.

The following month my daughter moved to Hawaii and began college in the dorms. We still had tension between us. October, I was able to bring my dog over. I arranged the service and did it. I didn't talk to My Marine about this. I didn't ask his thoughts or consider his perspective. I decided because I wanted to. Quite simply, I was still a bit salty and indignant about everything. It wasn't just him. I wanted what I wanted. At the time, I wanted to be selfish and get what I wanted without having to bend. Because of the current tension between us, I didn't discuss it with him first. I didn't want to contort myself for his comfort alone. He wasn't contorting for me. I knew if I had asked him, he would have said no. In retrospect, I was probably behaving indignantly and so was he. I can see that now.

It is possible the last straw for him was me negotiating the lease renewal for December with the landlord without discussing, it with him first. For this particular instance, he was aware that the landlord had stated when we first rented, that we could possibly have the rent lowered if we stayed for more than one year. So, in all honesty, when this was a problem for him, I was surprised. It shouldn't have been. The landlord and I had been communicating back and forth via email about it the renewal. When she and I agreed on the new reduced amount, I included My Marine in the email thread. When he saw the email, he called me from his room. When I came into the room, I remembered how visibly upset he was. From my perspective I was taking the initiative in handling business to lower our rent $1,200 a year but for whatever reason he didn't see it that way. He didn't like the fact that I had negotiated the lease with the landlord, and I hadn't spoken to him about it prior to agreeing to the new terms. He was upset that I told him after the fact by CCing him on the email. His reaction was as though I hadn't considered him at all and made a decision without him.

I saw a shift in him. I saw something that I hadn't seen since I had been in Hawaii. It might have been a glimmer of who he once was. Whatever it was, I was compelled to apologize immediately for not having a discussion with him before negotiating the lease, but I did apologize for not speaking with him first. He accepted my apology right away, but he then told me he wasn't going to sign the new lease. He later told a friend of mine that he was overwhelmed by a series of events, my daughter coming to college in Hawaii and then by me bringing my chihuahua. From July to November, it seemed as though any and everything I did upset him. In retrospect, there was actually more than those two things that he mentioned in that timespan. I didn't recognize it then, but it is quite possible that so much happening that quickly may have been overwhelming and extremely upsetting to him.

The Disconnect

This was late November 2022, the week before Thanksgiving, My Marine quietly gathered his things out of his bedroom, the air fryer and ice maker and left without saying a word. I woke up on that Saturday morning and he was gone. I was hurt. I was angry. I was confused. Within two weeks of our lease fallout, My Marine had moved out. It was on a Saturday without even telling me. I didn't understand how the conflicts seemed to keep snowballing. I had mixed emotions that day. On the one hand I was angry but there were also feelings of relief and indignation. It hadn't been going well between us at all the last few months, and nothing was being done to fix it. A few days later, he had texted me his new address. He also said that in time we would talk, and he would tell me why he left.

We still spent New Years together and exchanged our Christmas gifts. Peaceful time together again. Something we hadn't had in several months before he had moved out. Shortly after that, he began withdrawing from me again. When we discussed being intimate after we were no longer under the same roof, he said he didn't ever want us to fall into using each other like that if we weren't together. Especially being that I had asked if he had been seeing someone. I actually believed and trusted him and would rather be strong than shallow and superficial.

Throughout the year we were separated, I would always text periodically. I tried to give him space and not bother him, because I didn't want to press him. I wanted him to feel safe with me even though we weren't under the same roof. During this time, I did more research about attachment style, and I understood that he displayed dismissive avoidant behavior, along with PTSD. So, I deep dived into what that was and how to navigate his experience. I also looked into PTSD. It was a lot and even with me loving him as much as I did, it was a heavy burden. There were many times throughout that last year that made me want to give up on loving him. It was hard loving him and dealing with the realization that we weren't clicking. For the latter part of 2023, I had no hope that we were going to be able to fix things. There were times when I had to convince myself that our love was worth the work and discomfort. I would want him to do the exact same for me. It wasn't easy loving him from a distance while we were apart from each other.

I wanted to love, fight for, and be patient with him the same way I wanted him to love and fight for me. I didn't come here to Hawaii for a job or to be by myself. I came to Hawaii to be with him and to re-establish our relationship. I wanted us to be strong without outside influences of family and friends and build my new life. But in 2023 the year was so hard for me that I made the decision that he was worth it. We were worth it. He was worth waiting and being patient for.

When the first Valentine's Day rolled around after he had moved out, he still had a gift for me even though we weren't together anymore. Every year since he has been back in my life I have received a gift from him. I guess it's his way of showing me I'm special. He did not disappoint me, because I wasn't expecting anything. The tension between us was still there. During the first few months of our separation, I was very optimistic that he would come back home. Or at a minimum, we could re-establish our relationship even though we weren't under the same roof. I thought he just needed some space. We had had a rough few months, but we were greater than that. We just needed a reset. Our love was too great to not fight for.

Over the next few months, he didn't want to talk about him leaving. I went by his place once and we talked outside, but he was getting more and more distant. There was one time after he moved out that we were talking, and he told me about a time before he had moved that he was physically hurt because of his sciatica flare up. It had been that past August. I was trying to help him relieve the pressure from the knotted nerve. My Marine said that me trying to help him that day made him feel like I viewed him as helpless. In his words, this is the event that triggered him to push me away. He didn't want to be seen as helpless or needing anyone. He was doing fine by himself. During this conversation, he kept insisting that he had been doing fine without me and didn't need me.

    I only saw him a handful of times. Whenever I texted or called, he would respond right away. I was never ghosted or ignored, but I still gave him his space. I didn't show up unannounced to his place or swing by his office randomly, even though we were only a quarter of a mile away from each other. I was always considerate of his triggers. Throughout the year, I reached out less and less. I would ask if he was seeing someone else, and he always told me no. I felt like he was trying to create space, and it was becoming tiring for me to try and stay connected. It made me angry, and it was hurtful. There were so many times I had to convince myself not to give up on him because I didn't want him to give up on me.

    In December 2023, I moved into a smaller apartment since it was clear My Marine wasn't coming back. By this time, my messages to him were sporadic, and the last message I had sent was birthday wishes. I was completely unsure of what, if any, future was possible between us. So, I decided to make one last attempt to mend what was broken. Either he would respond or not, and I would move forward accordingly. I decided to send him a card with my spare keys, inviting him to a Valentine's dinner. In the card, I gave the time for dinner and how to enter my building with the security keys. For the remaining time of December and January, I was continuously looking for the card and keys to be returned in the mail. I never received anything from him, no calls, no texts. When February came, I was still looking for the card and keys to be returned in the mail.

During this time, I was praying to God to fix what was broken between us. I prayed for him, and I prayed for myself. There were times during February when I thought that since I hadn't heard from him, I'd told myself not to bother with dinner, but then I would keep the faith. My thought process was that even though I had not heard from him, I could choose to plan as though he was coming or stop planning the dinner. The "what if's" would cross my mind. "What if he showed? What if this is our last shot?" I told my friends that I was just going to prepare the dinner and if he showed up, great. We had a possibility to fix what was broken, and if he didn't, it was clearly the end of our story, but at least I had tried. At least I didn't give up on him.

Valentines fell on a Wednesday. February 14th came, and I still had not heard from My Marine, but I continued with the plan. So, I did go to work but left early so that I wouldn't be rushing to prepare dinner by five thirty that evening just in case he showed up. I went home to begin dinner and a few hours later, I received a text confirming the time for dinner. To express the excitement, I felt at seeing his message cannot be minimized. He remembered! He was coming to see me! I did have a lot of excitement. I quickly calmed myself, because I realized he could be coming simply to return my apartment keys to me. Then I received another text asking me was I still using the phone he had given me while we were together. I was so happy that I was going to see my baby again! From the time I had received his text that afternoon he was coming, I had to come down from my cloud nine and give myself a reality check. I put on my new dress and prepared myself to greet him. I remembered, he might just be coming to say goodbye and return the keys. So, with that in mind, although I had drinks in the refrigerator cooling, I had all the excess by the door so that he could take it with him. If he wasn't coming back, I didn't need to have his favorite beers or whiskey in the

Revenge of a Broken Heart

apartment since I don't really drink. Either way I knew this would be the beginning or this would be our end.

I received another text that he was going to be late, he had dozed off after work. He arrived about 20 minutes late. When I greeted him at the door, he came with a Valentine's gift. My new high-tech phone. I wasn't expecting that. We hugged, kissed, ate dinner, and talked for hours. Although the lobster was broiled a little too long, we had a great time! He did most of the talking. Mostly telling me about all the things that had been happening to him in recent months. He told me he had been in a fender bender, how he had let his temper flare in an incident, the new car, updates about his mom. It was as though he hadn't been talking and sharing with anyone. He shared so much. It felt like old times.

Being that I was an older, I knew how important was to ask direct questions, so that is what I did. At some point, I did ask if he was seeing anyone or dating, and he told me that he wasn't. He shared that he was doing the same thing as before and just taking care of himself. I felt relief that there was still a chance for us. At some point, I was massaging his temples and brows. It was something that I used to do when we used to live together. It always was a stress reliever for him, and it was nice to be able to bring him peace and comfort again.

I told him about my upcoming business trips to Alabama and Florida and asked if he wanted to join me. We discussed tourist attractions for the Alabama trip, and he quickly said "no" because there wasn't much to do. We sat, laughed, and talked for over five hours. As we sat and talked My Marine told me he was fixing dinner the next time. He was going to show me the best way to make red potatoes. He said mine were underwhelming. When we realized how late it was and that we both had work in the morning he prepared to leave. I told him he could take the beers and whiskey if he wouldn't be back. I said this to give him an "out" if he had wanted this to be our end. I didn't know another way to ask. He told me right then without hesitation that he was coming back. He took most of the beers but left the bottle of whiskey. When I walked him out to the security door it was after ten thirty, and we'd had a lovely, mature dinner date. Nothing was rushed or awkward. It was important to me to have a date and not move too quickly. It was a great night. There were future plans for us. The next day we messaged back and forth about how nice of a time we had had the night before. I felt relief. We were going to be okay. We could rebuild our foundation. This was our new start.

Over the next few weeks, we communicated with each other just about every day. One day while I was at work, I sent him an email. I said to him that we might as well get married since we knew we belonged together and that we could figure out the logistics of living together later. I had never felt that I couldn't share my thoughts and feelings with him. At the core of our relationship, he was my friend, and I still trusted him with everything. Since arriving in Hawaii, I had always told him that I wanted to get married before we left. Following the email exchange, I looked into how to get married at the Honolulu courthouse. As soon as I got the details, I emailed him the information. Following that, he told me we were too young to get married. He also said that when he was ready there would be no hesitation. About that I had no doubt. I reiterated to him again that I wanted us to get married while we were in Hawaii before the conversation ended.

When I received the details about my business trip to Florida, I asked him again if he wanted to join me and go to Universal Studios. He said that maybe we could do it when he retires in about two years. During these months, we consistently texted back and forth and even had planned for him to come over. On one particular Friday, he was supposed to come by after working a long shift. He wasn't going to be off from work until about 10pm. I was already in bed and had dozed off waiting for him. He never came over. The next day when I reached out to find out what happened, we went back and forth about it. He was really indignant and argumentative. This wasn't like him. I couldn't tell what the disconnect was about. My Marine said that he felt like he was being chastised by me. I wanted to understand why he was a no show, then mad about me questioning why he didn't at least call. Something wasn't clicking, and I couldn't figure out what it was. I was told that he went straight home because it was late. His behavior was noticeably defensive, but I honestly dismissed it as him just being tired and cranky for working overtime for the week.

For whatever reason, our connection and chemistry weren't working without us seeing each other face-to-face and I knew it. I was beginning to think he was avoiding seeing me in person. It seemed as though as long as he stayed away from me, he could resist me. Energy doesn't lie. I know I felt the chemistry and connection was still there between us. When we had our Valentine's dinner, things had seemed to be positive, and then the push back began again, but I was being patient. I didn't like the distance that creeped back in. Every time we made plans to see each other, he came up with an excuse at the last minute. It was like he was avoiding me. He wasn't picking up the phone -- only responding by text.

He was pushing me away. This went on for the entire month of April. I wondered if he felt as though he was weak if he was around me. I have no idea.

At the beginning of May, after a full day of texting back and forth about random things, he texted, "I don't think we can be friends." I had no idea what prompted this text. We had been getting along fine, communicating in a positive way. He went on to tell me that I needed to open myself up to someone else. I questioned if there was someone else in his life because in the three years he had been back in my life, he had never said anything like this to me before. He told me there wasn't anyone. My Marine said that we couldn't be friends because I would think it could lead to something more and it wouldn't. I was told that he still loved me, but he wasn't in love with me anymore. I honestly didn't know how everything could have taken a turn like it had, but I still had faith in him and in us. I believed that whatever wasn't clicking between us anymore, maybe time and space would heal it. I agreed to no longer be friends.

This made me sad, but I knew he wasn't responding to me the way he used to. He was closed off. I couldn't make him show up for me how I wanted him to if he didn't want to. So, I decided that I would give us six months of no contact and reach out to him in maybe September or

October. By that time, I would have achieved my glow-up. That was something I wanted for myself, and it was also something that was really important to him too. If by that time we still weren't clicking, then at least I had tried and gave it my best effort because he meant that much to me. Over the years, I had told him "Fair exchange is no robbery" and I meant it. If being my best physically is what he needed for us to have the love and life that I needed, it would be worth it. So, I went on a weeklong work trip and visited Universal Studios without him. I didn't know it at the time, but that text exchange was me getting dumped and cast away. I didn't even know it.

Pain and Betrayal

During my business trip, I was able to see and visit my friend Alexandra in Georgia. I hadn't seen her since I had moved to Hawaii. During that visit, I shared with her everything that had been going on with my relationship with My Marine. I confided in her that I would rather wait a few months and try again, over beginning to date other people. As for my friend, she didn't particularly like it or even agree. She understood the love that I had for him and was supportive of me. I told her, "If I reach out to him in a few months and it isn't clicking between us, then I will move on."

I was back from my work trip sitting in my apartment scrolling through social media. I then see pictures of him on his mother's social media page with a woman in a white dress. I didn't know what to think. I was confused. It was graduation season, so it was possible he was taking a photo at someone's graduation. I didn't know her, and they were standing close together like a couple. If you are confused, imagine how I could possibly have been feeling in that moment. Who is this person standing there holding onto him? He didn't come with me to Florida. Where is he? Maybe it's nothing. What is going on? All of these questions and thoughts sped through my mind. As I'm looking and scrolling on the media page, I see the face of the woman that was on his mom's social media page, and she had his last name.

Yes, what you are thinking happened, happened. The man that I had moved across the country to be with. The one I had been patiently waiting for, that I spent time, effort and energy attempting to understand him and his PTSD. The one I was committed to for the past three years, looked like he chose to get married to someone other than me. I didn't have the composure to use my voice and try to call him. I didn't have the strength to talk. I sent a simple text to him: Wow! As always, he responded to me immediately but this time with two question marks. I sent the screenshot of the picture of him with the woman in the white dress.

The devastation and heartbreak I felt was almost immediate. I have always known how much I loved him. The feeling in my body was gut wrenching. The pain in my chest throbbed. The tears streamed down my face. I would never have expected him to do anything like this to me. I was convinced and had believed that My Marine had an undying, unwavering love for me. This time the pain was worse than when we were young. I thought it was going to be our forever. We were older, more experienced, and more knowledgeable. I have never doubted him. I was locked in, loyal and committed, still. I wasn't perfect, but I never quit on him. My Marine and I went back and forth via text for about two hours. Struggling to express my hurt and explain why this hurt me. I sat there with tears streaming down my face. I was helpless. I didn't know what I could do. I didn't know what I should do. I was devastated.

Up until that very moment, I had never doubted how much My Marine had loved me. On so many occasions he had told me how much he loved me and that I was safe with him. I sat there numb. He messaged me that I never made moves to be his wife. That text alone knocked the wind out of me. My Marine had hurt me again. I was definitely hurt and angry with My Marine. I didn't feel any animosity to the Woman That Was Not Me. This was his doing and his choice in behavior. She was innocent in this. She didn't know me, and I was sure she didn't know about us. I didn't know who she was or where she came from. All I knew was that he'd told me on more than one occasion in the last few months and weeks that "there is no one else. I'm not dating."

Of course, when I found out about her, I wanted to know who this woman was who seems to have taken my place. I took the time to see her and concluded that she was a 20 to my 80. That is what I saw and believe. Despite me having 80% of desirable qualities, My Marines priority was maybe having the 20% of what I didn't have. I guess I'll never know. I have always been a girl's girl, but in the heat of the moment I felt that she needed to know who I was if she wasn't already aware. So, I sent her a direct message. The message sent was straight forward and kind. Was I being intentional in making myself known? Yes. As far as I was concerned, she got the man, I gave a congratulations and the issue was between My Marine and I, not her. However, I never attacked her on any level. The message I sent her asked no questions and required no response. Nor did I in any way blame someone I didn't know. She didn't deserve that. This betrayal was his doing.

A few days later she sent a personal attack with her words. It was unwarranted, uninformed, and disrespectful. I can understand her being upset, however, I never lied about anything I said because that is not who I am. At my core, I am an honest and direct person. I will continue to be just that, but the attack gave me every right to defend myself and I did. The Tortoise advised me to "get myself together mentally and physically." She was rude, disrespectful and that response was uncalled for, and it has solidified my belief that she is merely a 20 to my

80 as a quality person. When I sent my response message, I waited six hours to allow her to respond, which she did not.

The Tortoise may be an amazing person. I have no idea. Once I found out everything, I checked out her social media pages. I can tell you; she and I are absolutely nothing alike. If anyone ever says you can't read a person by social media they're lying. Generally, our pages reflect who we are and the image of who we want to portray ourselves to be. From what I saw of her on her social media page profiles that had a multitude of bikini pics and lobster licking. This was on all her platforms. She tends to lean into the physical appearance of her body and external validation. I was done with her. Any slight that I give her is due to her being so disrespectful in that message. Now, I can confirm that My Marine I knew back in the day and The Marine of my fifties liked a nice body. Absolutely. Most people do and there is nothing wrong with that. Generally, we recognize that physical traits are not the highest priority as we age. I believe that is maturity.

I just knew she wasn't me. Of my internet dive research of the Lobster Licker, there was nothing that revealed to me that gave the impression that she was equally yoked to my Ex-Marine. It gave me the impression that he is a level up for her and a clear downgrade for him in comparison to me. Clearly, she and I are absolutely nothing alike. There is a distinct difference in the caliber and substance between us. He hasn't changed that much in the last thirty years in what he finds appealing. To my detriment, I believed he loved me, I didn't realize how much it was still the same. In the same vein, The Marine I knew also had a jealous streak and like most men he didn't want to be threatened. So, a certain level of respectability was important to him, or at least it used to be. Or he only felt that way about me. It seemed that the woman he chose countered and didn't align with his protectiveness that I knew of him. I know that if I had ever portrayed myself so open and free to other men it would have been a problem for him.

One time, I shared with him about a specific man that. approached me on multiple occasions requesting my number and how upset he had become despite me telling him how uncomfortable and scary it was when that guy sought me out trying to get my number while shopping. I cannot see him having changed that much within the last year, but I guess I will never know. My Marine was very protective of me and did not like anyone looking at me, so the difference and comfort with his now significant other out for the world to see is astounding to me.

After he and I had our text exchange, he blocked me on one social media platform, but I could see he was watching on another of my pages. In consideration that he had not felt the need to tell me about what he did or block me; it was possible to surmise that his relationship with the new woman could only be successful if he blocked his own access to seeing me come across his News feeds. The first few days after finding out he had gotten married, I had really hoped he would come back to me, apologize, and tell me that he had made a mistake. I loved him and he loved me.

I wanted him to fix this, to have said or done something to take the pain away. I didn't want to believe that he would have hurt me. I began posting messages in my profile daily, just for him specifically. A few days later, I think what got him to block me was the message: "You did what you did. I felt how I felt. We said what we said. "Now leave me alone." He had told me in the past that he has always looked for me over the years and kept up with where I was. With social media, it is much easier to do if that is his intention. I do know that he chose to block me, even though he was the one who had been stalking my page.

After those messages, I didn't see any more of his profile name popping up on my notifications of profile views. He and I hadn't called or texted each other since he mailed my apartment keys to me. Initially, I had blocked the Not So Sharp Knife's page also, but eventually I unblocked her. I believe that if a person has the gall to look to see what I am doing, they can be in the front seat to see me win. At this point, I am thinking it is done. Anything that had to be said between us had been said. If I was too much, then he had gone on and found his less.

The pain and betrayal were devastating. It hurt so badly. I had truly believed that we were meant for each other and belonged together. I cannot speak for him, but I know I loved him for all of the right reasons. Him doing this made no sense to me. I couldn't align the words, the energy, the history, or the actions to come to the conclusion that he did not love me with his whole heart. How could he have possibly loved me for over thirty years of his adult life and then choose not to fight for me? To fight for us? To not choose me? The reality of it all is that I will likely never understand what happened to our love. I had been missing him throughout the past year when he had moved out.

Many times, over that year, I had to encourage myself to continue to wait for him and I did. I remained loyal and committed while waiting for him to be ready for us to try again. By doing that, I missed the possibilities of meeting someone else who was ready and sure about me. My life was completely on hold waiting for My Marine in which I was receiving no hugs, no kisses, no love. As far as I believed, no one understood us like we understood each other. None of that mattered. Now, all that was left was for me to gather my feelings, emotions, and make it through my life alone. My Marine and I were done. We had reached the end of our love story.

He never even uttered that he was sorry or remorseful for not telling me or any pain that was caused. He didn't care enough about me as a friend to even share that he was dating, or to even warn me that he'd moved on. He has had absolutely no accountability for his actions. The thoughts of what I could have missed or how I didn't know have ravished my mind. Even questioning myself about why I trusted him. The reality is, I did trust him. I trusted him in a way that anyone should be able to trust someone they love and who loves them in return. I had trusted him with everything. I had believed, if nothing else, I was safe with him. My heart, my feelings, my mind, body, and soul were supposed to be safe with him. When I went back through my text thread, the last time he told me he loved me first was July 2023. I believed that our love was special, sincere, genuine, and real. Could I have really been wrong about him all along?

Years ago, I had heard the story about Richard Pryor and Pam Grier. For those who aren't familiar, years ago they had been a couple. So much so that people who knew them were aware of how much they loved each other. One particular day, a colleague had been told that Richard had gotten married and was expecting to congratulate him and Pam. To his surprise, Richard Pryor had married a different woman that the colleague wasn't aware of. The colleague also knew that Pam was crushed behind the breakup. I remember thinking I couldn't imagine how he could have done that to her. The thought of one day you are loving and are loved by someone, and the next, they mean nothing to you. I don't think I will ever understand how My Marine could have treated me this way. Was he hiding everything behind his PTSD as an excuse this whole time? The questions torment my mind trying to comprehend.

    I truly believed My Marine loved me and parts of me still love him. There are some days that I believe that he still is in love with me and always will be. He assured me that his love for me was real and sincere. He had convinced me that it always had been. I never doubted it, at least not until now. He was my person and my emergency contact here in Hawaii. Unfortunately for me, I don't think I could have ever been more wrong in my life. To trust him. To believe in him. Parts of me think that it is impossible to love someone so deeply and then turn it off as though they meant nothing to you. He spoke to me like I was nothing. He moved on from our relationship as though I never even existed. How is that even possible?

My friends were really concerned about me during this time because they knew I came here to be with him, and I had no one here on the island except him. I was alone and they felt as though he had abandoned me. I would have never come to Hawaii had it not been for him. My friends were hurt that I was hurting. They were angry that he would hurt me like this.

The first few weeks after this bombshell of knowledge, I was having a really, really hard time dealing with this. I was devastated. This was what being heartbroken is. This is what it felt like. I had never been heartbroken before. Not even when our relationship ended when we were young. My mind was going a mile a minute, non-stop of what happened, what didn't happen, day and night.

"What did I miss?"

"How did I not know he didn't love me?"

"How could he do this to me?"

I know I was his Baby. I know he loves me. There is no way he didn't love me. This couldn't be real.

"Who was she?"

I have always asked him direct questions. There is no way that I could have missed something this important.

"How could he lie to me?"

He couldn't have loved me. There is no way that he could have loved me and did this to me.

"Why did he lie to me?"

"How could he have lied to me for three years?"

"His family, his friends, his therapist, none of them told him to tell me?"

"How could he do this to me?"

Over, over and over these questions and thoughts churned in my mind. I had thought at our core we were friends. Real, genuine friends that actually liked each other as people. I was having a difficult time functioning during the day. I would go to work, and tears would start falling from my eyes. I was in bad shape. I couldn't sleep. I couldn't eat. There were a few days I went into work but had to leave early because if I looked at the text thread or the picture, I would get physically ill. I eventually had to take some time off of work. I was having a difficult time being strong. I couldn't keep the mask up. My happy mask kept slipping. I was a complete wreck.

On one of those rough days, I called out from work. This morning, my friend Karina asked me for his telephone number. At one point she had said that she felt hurt and surprised by all of this and these events too. She said to me that she felt hurt and surprised by this. She wanted to talk to him, so she called him. After Karina called him that afternoon, she then called me to share the details of the conversation. I was told that he had taken the day off too. She expressed to me that he was very nice and had explained to her that we weren't a couple as though he was trying to clarify what our relationship status had been. My Marine professed to her that he had "moved on" from the relationship with me when he had moved out of the apartment in November 2022. When she repeated his words "move on," I became extremely upset all over again. It reminded me of what I had said to him over thirty years ago. "Kevin, move on!" The words rattled me. They had come back to haunt me.

Had I hurt him that intensely so many years ago, that all of this was his way of getting back at me for his pain? I didn't know what to think. Over the previous year, I had asked him on more than one occasion what he was doing and what he wanted to do. I had always asked him direct questions to get direct answers, which he always did. Right away without hesitation. I had always been told there was no one else. I never thought he would lie to me. We had said we wouldn't lie to each other. If he had told me he was seeing people or dating, I would have let him go. I would have known to protect myself. If he had said those words to me. "I'm moving on" I could definitely have made other choices.

My interpretation and understanding now is that he was just being selfish by not telling me. Maybe he got joy or security out of knowing someone was waiting for him. Maybe he liked knowing that I was ready to jump in and give love and attention if he needed it. I don't know. I suppose I will never know what his true intentions were. One thing I do know is that I didn't deserve this treatment. In a way that I would have never treated him. I know the history that we shared and his knowledge that I was waiting for him should have been enough for him to consider my feelings. Under no circumstances should a person knowingly lie and hurt another person. It's mean and selfish. Telling me would have been the considerate thing to do. The kind thing to do. The moral thing to do. He walks around and says that he's a Christian and he's a good, nice person, but then he still chose to mistreat me. We know the difference between right and wrong. His dishonesty with me wasn't good and the behavior wasn't kind.

Over the next few weeks, I started to do better emotionally. I was still emotionally spent, but I was able to function at work as normal again. I was beginning to recover, heal and function again. I had concluded that My Marine had made this choice because this person would require less of him. So, I was still broken hearted, but I had come to the conclusion that My Marine did still love me, but he made a choice for someone who required less of his mind, body, and spirit than I would. He wouldn't have to be vulnerable with her, like he did with me. Our history gives me a knowledge and awareness of him, that she can never have which equates easier. She will never know the intricacies of him that I have known and will never be able to comprehend the then and the now of us.

To my surprise, in the beginning of July about six weeks later, on one of my social media accounts, I noticed his Off-brand bride was viewing my Daily Stories on my social media page. Each time I saw this; I took a screen shot. After about three days of seeing her on my views I edited on two of the screenshots "Why? This is not a good look for you!" and posted it on my stories for her to see. My thought process was that since she wants to stalk my page, I'll give her something to see. I wanted it to be clear, I could see her watching. Late that evening, on the 4th of July, I received a text from the Marine. He said he reached out because I posted the screenshots of her stalking on my page. My initial response was "Why are you reaching out to me?"

This was absurd. Basically, telling me that I am warring with his passport bride. Him coming at me like this was a surprise since she was clearly stalking my page, not vice versa. Based upon the analytics on one of my social media platforms, she is still checking my page. After our last exchange in May, I hadn't reached out to him, and he hadn't reached out to me. We were done. There had been absolutely no communication between us, but this is why he reaches out to me? Initially, I sent a quick snap back asking why he was texting me. I sent a picture of the Lobster Licker bride that I had screenshot from one of her social media platforms where she had been tonguing a lobster. I told him in that message he and the "trash ass" deserved each other and they could both stay in the gutter. The sheer audacity for him to have the gall to reach out to me for this was infuriating to me. How dare he after all that he had done to me?!

After about two hours of fuming, I sent another response text. He and I texted back and forth in 100s of texts between the fourth and July 6th. I had been on vacation these few days, so I had nothing going on but texting with him. When I realized that I was emotionally drained by going back and forth with him, I finally blocked his number after my last message. By the time I blocked his number, I was emotionally exhausted with all of the back and forth between us. I realized I was defending and explaining myself to someone who didn't want me. To someone who chose to move on with their life without me and the hurtfulness of doing it without being honest with me. He did this without any regard for me. These two days of back and forth pushed me into a tailspin. We were no longer anything to each other and I believe the biggest disappointment outside of his failure to be honest with me was the knowledge that he never took the opportunity to fix whatever was broken between us.

TL Phillips

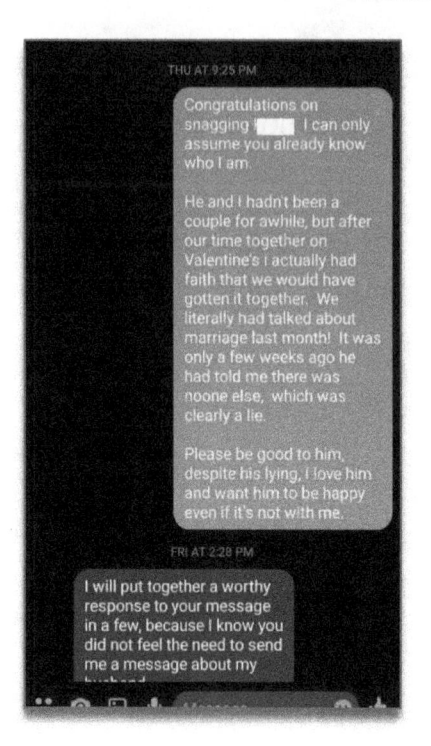

> **THU AT 9:25 PM**
>
> Congratulations on snagging ▮▮▮. I can only assume you already know who I am.
>
> He and I hadn't been a couple for awhile, but after our time together on Valentine's I actually had faith that we would have gotten it together. We literally had talked about marriage last month! It was only a few weeks ago he had told me there was noone else, which was clearly a lie.
>
> Please be good to him, despite his lying. I love him and want him to be happy even if it's not with me.
>
> **FRI AT 2:28 PM**
>
> I will put together a worthy response to your message in a few, because I know you did not feel the need to send me a message about my husband...

> The level of self control it has taken me to not disrespect you is beyond the ordinary. Woman go fix your self mentally and physically. You have some serious deep rooted psychological issues that need to be addressed. It's rather pathetic to see a woman that tries so hard to solicit allies to win a Man's heart. If he has expressed to you in so many ways, that you are not his type and he does not want/see a future with you, at what point will this resonate with you mentally. You are not a part of our story and never will be......That being said; "Keep my husband's name out of your mouth." Kevin, is married, happy, in love, is being loved correctly and has found his person. Go fix yourself and find your peace.

> He lied that you even existed.
>
> ▮▮▮ has been a blessing to me and I have been a blessing to him. If you think my coming here to be with him didn't crack open his heart again, you are mistaken. He was pretty much a recluse when I came back in his life. I challenged him to be a better version of himself. Based on your comments/reaction, you believe a narrative that doesn't exist.
> I am a woman of substance and will always be seen as Beautiful, Amazing and Caring by your now husband. Even if he is mad that I spoke up, I will forever be his First Love. Essentially, I am the 80 to your 20 no matter how he spins it.

154

Hit Dogs Will Holler

Some of the things that he said on the text thread hurt so much, and they continuously ring in my mind. "I never wanted a relationship with you. I never wanted anything from you. You are overbearing and entitled. I never wanted your love. You were never the only one. I always had options. I told you OVER, OVER, and OVER. You aren't my type. I never wanted anything from you. When you picked me up from the airport and I saw you I didn't think it was going to work out but for me to say it wouldn't have been nice. Me and my brother-in-law both said you were crazy when you forced yourself to pick me up from the airport. My aunt told me my wife was for me. No one in my family or friends wants to deal with you. They don't know if you are dealing in reality. You never made moves to be my wife. I would have never chosen you. One time when we were intimate, I reached around and grabbed belly, and it was a turn off. It wasn't about PTSD, it was you. I didn't want to be with YOU. Sex with you was nothing memorable. I can get sex anywhere."

Were these the words of a hit dog hollering, or were these words the truth of his feelings for me? The most devastating and hurtful thing that he expressed was when he said I never made moves to be his wife. All of these words felt like an arrow through my heart. It was so painful it took my breath away. As far as I am concerned, uprooting my life and spending thousands of dollars to get here to start a new life with him was that "ultimate" move to be his wife. My move to Hawaii should have been evidence of wanting to be his wife and aligning my life with his that he never would have doubted my intentions. Every effort I made was because I intended to be with him forever.

Like a fool, every time he said he wasn't ready for a relationship, I believed it was about PTSD. It made no rational sense for him to say he was in love with me, think I am amazing, smart, beautiful, and all of the complimentary labels he has given me over the years; to then say I am not his type because of my size. Prior to our split when he moved out, I could say he told me over and over that he wasn't ready for a relationship, but at no point when we had our Valentine's dinner or after, had he said anything like that.

Everything about this situation hurt me. It hurts because we had a relationship that he minimized to having been nothing to each other. The Marine knew I was waiting for him to be ready over the past year we were apart. He basically denied everything that we were to each other -- every loving exchange and has treated me like I was nothing and never have been. He has since told my friends that he allowed me to come to Hawaii because he was such a nice guy. As though making all those efforts, spending the time, money, and effort to relocate had nothing to do with the two of us. He denied this to my friends as though I was nothing. Anyone who has critical thinking skills would know this was untrue. People who knew me and were a part of my journey, he said this to them as though he was some missionary doing God's work. That wasn't our life. After we got back together, I never doubted his love for me. I believed he was in love with me, my girls did, my family did, and my friends did. So, his words were stabbing. Based on that foundation of love that I thought we had, I would have never thought he would have been cruel or venomous to me. I deserved more respect than that. Now I can't say I didn't say some things that might have been hurtful as well. It is quite possible that what I said is looping in his mind too. I did want to hurt his feelings. I was intentionally mean in return, but it wasn't vicious in my opinion. I didn't try to break him like he did me. Even in the end, I cared too much. In our last exchange of texts, I had become the hit dog hollering:

"You criticize me for my size, but you look about five months pregnant. I've seen her social media; you aren't even her type. She's going to cheat on you. She's only using you to get to her next man. Your oral is trash! Women want to climb the walls with pleasure and because you used to have a nice body and a big member you think that you don't have to do anything. You're a selfish lover. She's gutter trash and you can stay in the gutter right with her. I'm definitely too good for you. You and your Only Fans bride deserve each other. You two are on your Passport Bro honeymoon but stalking my social media accounts. You two are pathetic!"

I was told that the Woman That is Not Me, is his type and it would have been unfair to me for him to try and force me to be that type of woman. I honestly thought I was his type all of these years. I recognized I wasn't the healthiest (BP, A1C numbers used to be all over the place) and my best shape, but I was continuously working on it. At one point during this conversation, My Marine said to me that I had two years since being in Hawaii to get it together and that when I didn't, it showed him that I wasn't serious, which didn't work for him. From my perspective, he showed me no grace and he definitely didn't show any concern about what was going on with me medically. I had believed I was his type. He had convinced me of that. I had believed that I was everything he could ever need or want in a loving partner. Although I wasn't where I wanted to be aesthetically, I wasn't so far removed from it that he should have been okay with letting me go and not working things through. Looks and bodies change for all of us.

This exchange in July ripped open the scar that had begun to adapt and heal from his betrayal in May. I was in agony all over again. I was initially hurt and devastated but this time was worse because he chose to be disrespectful, nasty, and rude to cement his disdain for me. I now had to heal from the callous, mean, and hurtful things told to me. It was no longer a betrayal; it was a full-blown attack on who I was. Any vulnerability or sensitivity that I had shared during our relationship was used to cause me pain. I hadn't seen that level of his nastiness in over 30 years. It was still in him; he had just chosen not to show me that side until now.

I also felt I lost not only him, but his family as well. I didn't know all of them, but those I did know, I loved. I had wanted them too. I wanted to be an aunt to his nieces and nephews, a sister to his siblings, and a daughter to his mother. Knowing and believing that it was God who brought us back together so seamlessly, I will never believe that God told him to marry the 20 to my 80 without giving the discernment that he would need to tell me for protection. God has always blessed me and has revealed things to me. Even at times when I didn't have the maturity and understanding of those revelations. I truly believe that stumbling across that picture of My Marine as a couple, was a reveal. This may have been God preparing me for better because he knows I would have continued to have wasted time, energy, and effort on this love.

I don't think I'll ever truly understand why our relationship has ended this way. In some ways I guess My Marine was "bread crumbing" me the entire time. Maybe keeping me as an option. His not directly answering if he was seeing someone else created a hope that he was just working on himself, by himself. During the year when he moved out, I asked him several times if he was starting to date. The answer was always no. You may wonder why I didn't assume there was someone else, or dating when we weren't having sex anymore, or even talking to each other on a regular basis. Simply because I trusted him. He had never given me a reason to think he was lying to me. I believed him because when we first reconnected, he had been celibate for two years already. So, for him to choose not to be sexually active wasn't a stretch for him. We were intimate only once after we no longer were under the same roof.

My friend Daryl asked me once what did I do for My Marine and I told him honestly. The only thing I ever did for My Marine was love and support him. I was his partner. I would do sweet things for him, but he didn't need me to cook or clean for him because he could do that for himself. He cooked for me more than I did for him. I offered and gave him unwavering love and support.

When I had told him back in 2021 that I would never leave him again, I was being honest. I sincerely meant it. I would not have left him. I came to Hawaii to build a life with him. Not change his plan. I only wanted him to include me in his plan, not alter it. All this time, I had wanted to get married because I didn't want to be his "special friend" if something were to happen to him. I wanted the commitment. I wanted to grow old with him. I realize now that because I trusted him so deeply that I expected that is what my life was going to be.

Once I was aware of what he had done, he told me he didn't have to tell me that he was dating. That he wasn't obligated to tell me anything. Technically that is true, but it definitely would have been what a good man would have done. It would have been an honorable thing to do. He knew I was waiting for him, and he knew I loved him.

I believed the level of sacrifice and love that I gave him should have been sufficient enough for him to be brave enough to have said, "I'm seeing people, someone, I'm getting married." I recognize that it would have been an uncomfortable conversation for me. The chaos was created by him because of his failure to say anything. He would like the world to view him as a nice or good guy, but that isn't what his behavior showed. He took the coward's way out.

In the pictures that I have seen of him, he looks different. He is dying his hair black now. I suppose he's trying to appear younger, or he's having a midlife crisis. He's lost a few pounds, so he no longer looks like five months pregnant. So that is good. Healthier for him, but even though he is smiling in the picture that I've seen, it doesn't seem sincere. Even though he is smiling, my first thought was, "Why can't you be who you are?" He is a 54-year-old man, about to be 55, dying his hair. In the last three years of me knowing him, he was wearing gray in his beard. The pictures seem performative, like "look at me, I'm so happy." I know I loved him for who he actually was, not for who I wanted him to be. The Marine's looks, money, or status weren't relevant to the love that I had for him. So that makes me sad for him. I recognize that he was unable to love me for who I actually was because of a preferred physical aesthetic, and now he is with someone who he maybe feels will not love him for who he actually really is at his core. That wouldn't be surprising though. With everything that has unfolded, my friends and I understand the brand of what his new wife's social media platforms exude. Most people who have similar backgrounds to me and discernment would interpret what we saw as a woman that moves in the Jezebel or Delilah spirit, which is very distinct and a clear presentation.

I had always thought he had a Dismissive Avoidant attachment style behaviors for the past three years. I had been researching and trying to understand this behavior all of this time. These last three years had been difficult, especially when he moved out, but I was committed to him and trying to be patient. One of my friends believes that he is a narcissist. Another one thinks that Caterpillar Brows put "roots" on him, while someone else believes he was just being a typical selfish man and other thinks that it boiled down to the fact that he wouldn't have been able to control me because of my career and finances. I don't know which one was accurate, some of them or if any of them were for that matter. I did know this pain and devastation was real, and it hurt. It was as though I had been physically punched in the chest. The intensity of trying to have a jaw dropping scream but not having the sound to voice it.

As all this fallout happened, I was continuing to work on my health, recovering from the depression, and making myself the priority. This included improving my medical numbers, shedding the weight I wanted, and not quitting on myself. My medical numbers and my weight were about me. Although my desire for him wanted him to see me as beautiful AND sexy inside and out, it seemed that my external beauty was more important. He once told me that physically was important because he needed to be attracted to his wife, so he wouldn't have to cheat to be satisfied. I didn't think much of it at the time because most people want to be physically attractive to their partner. I feel that way too. I know I have never been ugly, and I have never been so overweight that my attractiveness was hidden. I had never believed he wasn't attracted to me or didn't find me desirable. I had never believed I wasn't his type. I can beat myself up that I didn't drop the weight fast enough or maybe even if I had gotten the medicine in September instead of March, he would have seen my progress by our Valentine's date, and everything would have been different. This I'll never know.

As I have gotten older, I have become prone to fainting and dizzy spells. Because of that I generally always keep someone informed of where I am, in case of emergency. After I was discarded by My Marine, I had a few episodes of passing out and lightheadedness. It was upsetting not having him to call if I needed him or was scared. It is something that I had to deal with being on an island without my person. Having an episode did bring me to the reality that I could not remain in Hawaii alone. He was my person, my go-to, my emergency contact. If something were to happen to me, there would be no one to come to my aid or be able to speak for me. This experience resonates the saying of "No man is an island." But I was on an island with no one to come to my aid or rescue if needed. The reality is that everything happens the way it should, and people make their decisions based upon various things that may never be shared or didn't even happen.

In a conversation that we had weeks before finding out he had gotten married, My Marine said to me, "You are beautiful and amazing. If you got your body right, you would be the best." So here I am a few months later, being my "best" and he has chosen to get married to someone else. I just needed more time and grace. He should have loved me in the meantime. Without a doubt he should have loved me enough to show me grace and wait for me, just like I waited for him. Just like when we were in our twenties when I was able to wait for him. He should have waited for me. Fair exchange is no robbery.

The Marine has brought me this tremendous pain and betrayal trauma. I recognize it is more than just having my feelings hurt. This experience was nothing short of devastating to me. I truly believed coming here to Hawaii was a new chapter with the love of my life and we would attain our happy ending.

Our story ended more tragically than I could have ever imagined. When we reconnected, it was unexpected, invigorating, and flat out surprising. He convinced me he loved me. That he had always loved me and wanted a life with me to rewrite our story. After letting my guard down, I never doubted his love for me and what I meant to him. The trauma of experiencing a situation that makes you question your entire being of being a rational, emotionally stable healed person.

I find myself trying so hard to understand how he could have done this and be so callous towards me. I have concluded that I will never fully understand. I can only try to forgive myself for all that has transpired. In my Dreamgirls, Effie voice, "My Marine was supposed to love me!"

Even the thought of having never received an apology or any type of accountability has been hurtful. He told me that he didn't owe me any explanation or apology, and I wasn't his best friend. Situations and people change. I know that. Most of us are aware of this and have a level of understanding of that reality. However, I have always believed that if you really love someone, that you always will. Like it or not. How do you pine over someone for over thirty years to turn around and act like this? Either you never loved them, or you are acting as though they are nothing.

In the end, I had to find out that I was not the greatest love of his life, only his first love. I really wanted an apology. After I found out, I really wanted him to reach out to tell me he had made a mistake, and he knew we belonged together. I really, really wanted him to come back and fix this. I really, really wanted it to be a lapse in his judgment. Just a mistake of the flesh. With time, I came to understand that he knew what he was about to do during those conversations for the past few months. At our Valentine's dinner, he knew. When we were emailing about marriage a few weeks later and he said, "I'm in no rush to remarry," he knew. When I said, "You know we belong together; we might as well just do it and iron out the kinks later," he knew. Then three months later he gets married. He knew he had chosen someone else and that it would crush me. He knew and he didn't care.

To my shock and surprise, I no longer mattered to the man who I thought I was the love of his life too. I heard him every time he said he wasn't ready for a relationship and because I was trying to understand him and the changes he had gone through; I didn't view it as him not wanting me. Only as a "not right now, I can't do it. I'm not ready." It was never, "not you. I don't want you." I had believed that due to his own mental capacity that he wasn't able to love me how he or I had wanted currently, but that it wouldn't have been like that permanently. That he needed time to continue to get better. It never occurred to me that he just didn't want me. I believed he loved me and that being vulnerable was extremely difficult for him. There were so many times following our Valentine's date where he could have told me he was involved or dating, but he chose to lie to me. He lied in February. He lied in May. Repeatedly stating that there was no one else. While always knowing how I felt about him and that I was waiting and wanting us to work things out. No matter how it is rationalized, he made a decision to lie to me because he knew.

When things like this happen, it's so easy to compare yourself to the other person when in all actuality it has nothing to do with them. She and I are not the same. We're not the same generation, age group or caliber of woman. She and I are not the same and I could tell just by viewing her social media accounts. We are not comparable. Comparison is the thief of joy. I am a woman of substance with integrity and pride, but he hurt me. This had nothing to do with the other woman. At the end of the day, he chose her and not me. That is what matters to me. He didn't love me enough or have the capacity to love me properly in order to choose me. Again. He didn't choose me again. He chose someone else over me. Again. My Marine is no longer mine. I find it really difficult to believe that My Marine doesn't love me even now. I'm not sure if it is my ego or my heart that has me thinking and believing that. Right now, at this moment, I believe that My Marine probably truly loves me, and he just doesn't know how he can love me without losing himself within our love.

    Love is powerful and can be scary. Our love cannot be shallow or superficial. It requires intensity and a level of vulnerability that is not easy for him. When I came to Hawaii, I came to build a life with him. Because of where he was on his journey, I knew that I had to give selflessly of my time and energy to meet him where he was at. I know that he slowly progressed, but I never imagined that he would come to see me as a callous that he needed to shed as he grew on his healing journey. It is often said that we don't often know what we mean to people. I think in general most people assume that it means that we are of great importance to people, and we aren't aware of it. This experience has taught me that we in fact don't know what we mean to people. I would have never thought that even on our worst day that he would have treated me like this. Like I meant so little to him. In the end, he spoke to me so cruelly and venomous that there is no way to avoid the realization that either he was lashing out as a defense mechanism because he knew he was wrong, or that I meant nothing more than a tool to him that he utilized to get him to a better place mentally. I may always be his first love, but in his eyes maybe my existence creates disdain in him.

So, this is how it ends for our love story. Hawaii was a new chapter of my love story. I recognize that now. I just hadn't predicted that our chapter would end here.

It has been so easy to doubt things I have done or said. All of this was about a break in our relationship. He was not being honest with me and doing this was deceptive and selfish. As a result, it made me feel worthless. It tore open wounds that I had thought were long healed. The Marine replaced me and ignored what damage he created. This made me feel utterly alone. I have cried myself to sleep over this. Chances are he will never understand how much he has hurt me. It is even possible that he may never understand why the decisions that he made were hurtful. My presence, my existence, our history was reduced down to inconsequential nothingness by him. I was nothing to a man that I had believed in my heart of hearts would have moved mountains, swam oceans, and would have died for me if need be.

I wanted to be everything that he needed and wanted for life because he was everything that I wanted for life. Friends will tell a person when they're going through something like this, "You are enough. They were wrong. It doesn't matter." However, most people would take this as a punch in the gut and not understand why the person they cared for didn't care for them in the same manner. Emotions can take us in a whirlwind. For this to happen, I didn't feel like I was enough.

Don't get me wrong, once we connected, we had an active love making life. He never gave me a reason to doubt that he found me attractive or desirable. I knew he wanted me to be "hard core" in the gym because during most of his twenties and thirties, which had been his life. I did feel the pressure from him to be an active gym girly.

I worked out and swam for fitness even though doing gym workouts seemed in vain because I didn't know what I was doing. He had offered to cover the costs of CrossFit classes, but he never actually did it. All the while, he was a literal couch potato with a dad bod. I always felt it was unfair pressure because he had been clearly out of shape for years. So no, fitness was not my first priority. My funds were. When it came to him and me, the last piece of the puzzle that I didn't have was the body that would please him.

According to him, I am beautiful and amazing. He didn't care about my money, but I know he had told me how proud he was of my educational and career success. In theory, most men say they want a woman who makes good money, but in practice, it becomes a threat to some. They may view themselves as less needed by her if she is able to contribute financially in an equitable manner. I wonder now if it had become an issue that I regained my financial strength. After the first year, I was financially equal to him. Did he feel that I didn't need him to be the King anymore? I just don't know. I am trying to focus only on the positivity given. The negative is too damaging.

I am more than my body type. I am so much more. Throughout the past few years, one of my prayers had been asking God to heal and save him for me. I continuously read and recited from the Bible, "Love is patient. Love is kind. Love is enduring." These words helped me to keep the faith when I was attempting to love him. Not realizing I wasn't loving myself.

TL Phillips

Putting Myself Back Together

I have been told my entire life that I am a heartbreaker. I think that people assume that when you are conventionally attractive, you are just out in the world hurting people's feelings. That is the furthest thing from the truth. I have lived a very lonely life. Many people assume I have a multitude of friendships and relationships, but they just don't exist. I have always attempted to take another person's feelings into account. Being a presumptive "heartbreaker" doesn't negate a person having feelings, and it definitely doesn't mean to hurt them before they can hurt you. The strange part to me about this is that I've never broken a heart. I haven't even had a desire to be so hurtful to someone. But my heart has been, multiple times. I have always tried to consider others and yet no one has considered me in return. Until this recent heartbreak, I recognized the pain I felt before was hurtful and painful, but it was not a heartbreak. Heartbreak is more distinct. It has a painfulness that is felt in the mind, body, and spirit.

We all have something special about us. Sometimes people see it and sometimes they don't. No one that we meet in this world is random. I don't regret the love that I have had in my life. I don't ever regret the love I gave. Those I gave my love to probably and most likely needed it at the time. As with us all, every experience we have had has brought us to the place that we are today. The hits, hurts, and scars happened. I'm pretty sure that I will die believing that the love we shared was true and pure. At least it was for me. I will always have love for my Ex-husband and the Marine. Surely until the day I die. I cannot rationalize how I feel. I feel what I feel. I wish I could have done things differently and my stories would have ended differently. The most honest thing that can be said about this for me is that I don't want anyone who doesn't want me. It's possible they wanted the "idea" of me. Coming to terms that they didn't truly love or want me is heartbreaking, and there is nothing that I can do about it. I think of one of them constantly because it is so fresh. Wondering what was the moment that his feelings changed for me.

Sometimes you will hear women say that no one loves that man like they do. There is some truth to that because each of us loves differently. Some days, I believe that he and I failed because he showed me no grace. He wanted me to be perfect in every way. One of my friends asked me if I really would have taken him back after marrying someone else, and my honest answer was yes at the time.

When I first found out, it seemed unreal, unlikely, implausible that he could have done this if he was thinking straight because he has loved me for his entire adult life, and I was now hurting. If he had come to me and said, "I made a mistake. I'm getting it annulled. Let's fix this." I would have. I wanted him to fight for me, just like I would fight for him. He didn't fight for him. My ex-husband didn't fight for me. I wasn't important enough for either of them to fight for.

When I view us, I see us starting from a similar foundation and currently at a similar place in our lives with our successes. I recognize how we got to this point in our lives is different though. For him, he committed to the job which required mental and physical exhaustion. For me, it required earning degrees and mental exhaustion. Because of those differences our friend circles and lifestyles are only slightly different. I never thought much of this because I had believed the circle between him and me was the most important one, but after listening to the speaker Sadia Psychology there is a concept of "punching up or down" out of your dating weight class.

For all intents and purposes, this was never a consideration of mine, but according to the psychologist, this behavior is a real thing. If at any point your partner may feel that they are "punching up or down," it can be a threat to the relationship. Although I felt he and I were on equal footing, we were upgrades for each other in presence and substance, but for him and the Turtle, the upgrade is clearly only for her. So, I believe that maybe My Ex-Marine may have viewed me as out of his weight class. And rather than working on those insecurities he may have felt, he found someone below his own "weight class." I was waiting for him, and I had believed that he had loved me enough to give us another try. I had believed our Valentine's Day date was a step towards that reality. Unfortunately, I was wrong. I deserved better treatment from him.

As a child of God, I have always believed that we are tested to make choices (free will). I believe that during our break-up, the Marine was tested and tempted and failed that test. I find it extremely difficult to believe that God didn't bring us back together. I also find comfort in knowing that despite him leaving me the way he did, I was still okay. I didn't lose any progress that I had made since my divorce. I believe he made a choice without getting guidance from God because there is no way that there would have been this confusion. So, I believe that the Marine probably loves me still and unfortunately, he made a choice that he will have to live with. He had said he wanted our story to end better than it did. He said that if I was patient with him, he would make it right one day. Maybe he forgot all of that. If anything detrimental were to happen to me, I suppose the guilt would probably eat him alive.

I don't want anything to happen to him because I love him and will likely love him for the rest of my life. However, right now I don't wish him well. I don't wish the best for him. I hope that he one day feels the pain that I have felt just because I allowed myself to love him and opened myself to trust him again. Good or bad, he was my Clyde. Dumb or stupid, he was my Romeo. He has always been cemented as my Dwayne. I hope that the reality of how deep the love I had for him, one day hits him hard enough to knock the wind out of his chest. I am sure a day will come when I don't feel any animosity in my heart but today is not that day.

I still am healing from this heartbreak. My Ex-Marine has loved me for the majority of his adult life. He was supposed to choose me every day, even when times get hard. He did not do what he said he would. There is a small bit of comfort in knowing that he still loves me even though he has made this awful decision. There is a level of peace in knowing that I did not quit on him. I gave everything I could to love and support him when I came to Hawaii. Unfortunately for me, it seems that it was all a lie and I will have to contend with the fact all of the love and memories I thought we were sharing during our time since he came back into my life in 2020, was his only version of being a nice guy. He in fact wanted nothing to do with me, only to receive whatever I gave. I spent the last 4 years of my life believing I meant something special to someone when I actually wasn't anything of value to him.

Words that have resonated and that I am trying to absorb are "He didn't leave you for someone better. He didn't leave you for someone better looking. He left you for someone easier." He and I share a history that neither of us can ever repeat. We are each other's first love, and we will always be a part of each other's life story, but this will not be the end of love. I have a beautiful love to give. I know that the Lord wouldn't have given this desire of my heart, if there wasn't a love in the world for me, by someone who has the capacity.

I have felt this heartbreak in my heart, mind, and spirit. I recognize now that feeling heartbreak from a partner was new to me. Throughout my adult life there has been pain, lost love, sorrow, and disappointment. The pain of lost love and heartbreak are significantly different. I recognize that I have the capability to love deeply, and that love is nothing new to me. I am a lover at heart, so I love easily. Understanding myself, I recognize that I have only been deeply in love twice in my life. The first time I was in love, there was a level of naivety, boldness, and audacity on my side. When I walked away from love in my young adulthood, I perceived that there was more misery than love between us at the time. I assumed that all love would saturate us deeply. I was wrong. The boldness of my youth led to the belief that true love and connection were easy to come by. With time I learned that true love and connection is actually rare. I have remained grounded, and healing is my top priority.

So, with time I was humbled in what love really is for me. I learned that there will always be people that come around who may be more handsome, funnier, and more outgoing. Although there are people in the world that can be more exciting, it is important to not confuse excitement with love. Love must be there when there are exciting and boring times. It's the feeling of wanting to be around them still when there is nothing to say. For me, an indicator of this is if I can be completely comfortable with that person without having the need to "fill the air" with conversation or background sounds. Is there still comfort in the silence around us with the security of only our presence?

My friend Alexandra has once said to me, "God sometimes allows pain in order for us to get our blessings. God could see that you would have never left him, and it would have only caused you pain." I suppose that was something that I needed to hear because I had told him, "I would never leave you again" and I had meant it with my whole heart. I was locked in for life. She had responded, "Exactly. You would have never left him even though he had stipulations for your body but didn't have any for his own. This was God's protection over you. God had to let him walk away from you. Your Marine loves you. I promise you; he loved you as much as he could probably love anyone, but he has vices, Tina. He knows you deserve better because he has to work through them, if he ever does."

You see, I knew I had moved to Hawaii to be with him. It was me continuing my new life, with the love of my life. When I had chosen to wait for him, these were the thoughts in my mind. For the remaining years of my life to be with him. The life I wanted was for us to be in love together. I am grateful that I still believe in love. Love has never created fear for me, but it does now. If you love someone with all of you, someone can choose to not honor, respect, and appreciate that love. It makes us vulnerable to pain. What we intend for ourselves does not guarantee that someone will love you in return. Love should feel like the comfort of a warm, secure hug. I didn't believe I lacked awareness when dealing with my loves but maybe I was naïve. Naïve in thinking that love for me would not allow them to treat me the ways in which they did.

TL Phillips

We Reap What We Sow Letters

Psalms 40:14: May those who try to destroy me be humiliated and put to shame. May those who take delight in my trouble be turned back in disgrace. Let them be horrified by their shame for they said, "Aha! We've got him now!" But may all who search for you be filled with joy and gladness in you. May those who love your salvation repeatedly shout, "The LORD is great!"

Dear Ex-husband,

I attempted to be the best wife to you that I was able. I gave the entirety of my 30s and 40s to a life with you. You know the type of husband you were to me, and I wish that you would make the choice to do right for me. Even though our marriage was not a success story, I thank you for our family and all the positive things that you have done. Although there was a great deal of bad, I know you were also a blessing in ways as well.

Although I still have a level of bitterness and animosity within me in relation to our marriage, I do wish you the best that life has to offer you. I wish you happiness and love for your life.

Tina

The 20,

    The love that I have for you is limited to being a fellow child of God. Your involvement in my story is limited and this last bit of attention that I am giving you is attributed to your unnecessary, unwarranted disrespectful comments towards me. He doesn't see the conniving manipulation in you that I see but he should have warned you to sit this one out. I know that I am a girl's girl, so I hope you have been inspired based on how you have stalked my page. Although I am extremely nice, I also push back. I was raised as an East Coast American, so I look out for the young and respect my elders. It is evident we are not the same, so show some respect. The next time you have keyboard courage, just don't. You may have gotten the hardware, but I will always have his heart. I really thought he had evolved past his savior complex of hood booger types, but here we are. My only wishes for you are the following.

    May any disdain and disappointment with his life and our home of Hampton be revealed and show on your face. May he accidentally say my name when he's talking to you. May you wish I have a long and prosperous life because if something were to happen to me, you will not have the ability to console him.

Always the Solid 80

Revenge of a Broken Heart

Dear Heartbreaker,

You, your friends, and family were all great actors. I was convinced your love for me was true and that they were genuinely happy we were back together, but it seemed it was all lies. When you said you were committed to me, I believed and trusted you would do your part to give us our happy ending. I didn't deserve this betrayal or broken heart, especially since you claimed to have loved me for the last 35 years. All I had wished and expected was for you to fight for us again.

You attempted to diminish and discount my value because you don't know what your value is. You always talk about being a nice guy/good man, but you need to understand there is a difference between the two. Your behavior was reprehensible. You were a manipulator. There was nothing nice or good about your behavior or betrayal towards me. Your actions make you righteous and moral. I had believed you were a much better human than you actually are. You are wanting people to believe God told you to treat me that way is astounding.

I wish you had at least said to me one time, "I'm seeing other people." It would have given me the opportunity to make a different decision for myself. I wouldn't have moved into the new place with you. I likely wouldn't have stayed in Hawaii. You took all of these choices away from me.

Since Mariah Carey has been the playlist of our love story since the beginning, I wish you would think of me every time you hear any of those four songs.

Your Ex-Baby

The Takeaway

As you can tell, I am forever the optimist. I am beginning to see how although it should be a positive thing about me, it has allowed room for others to manipulate and gaslight me. It has caused me to stay longer in situations that I should have gotten out of.

So here I am again, attempting to gather myself up and telling myself to stiffen my backbone. To stand tall and keep pushing. I may be heartbroken, but I refuse to be broken. I have chosen to accept what is, acknowledge my part, heal the hurt, and move forward. There is no other alternative for me. I am absolutely ready for that hurt to not hurt me anymore. Sometimes adulting can be really, really hard. Being an adult requires that we have to get up each day and go to work, plaster a smile on, and keep going. No one sees your pain or knows your pain.

I was watching a video the other day when the psychologist mentioned that the fastest way to get over a heartbreak is to accept your part and be accountable that it is all of your fault that it happened. Her words were that doing this does not negate what had been done to you, but it allows you to accept that it is highly likely that you ignored red flags or did not uphold your own boundaries.

Boundaries that are meant to protect your heart and mind. After contemplating her words and thinking over what my life had been with both My Ex-Husband and the Marine, there were definitely times in which I put their needs ahead of myself. More times than I prefer to even acknowledge. There was a time that both of these men wanted me without question. They wanted me to be a huge part of their lives, and at some point, their hearts and minds changed about me. They will both tell you that they wanted me to be their wife at some point. It seems to me that way too often men want me when they first get to know me. As time progresses, it seems as though they want to conquer me. Then over time, maybe they wanted me to humble myself or be less than what I am. As though my light may shine just a little too bright for them. In all reality, I shouldn't have to humble myself to show them I'm not a threat because they are scared of me. I'm not a threat unless you are a threat to me. That is the case for most people. We all have a light, and some people seem to shine more brightly than others.

    This chapter in my life I am healing and learning to better understand myself and the boundaries that are necessary for my own security. Having boundaries doesn't take away the possibility of having your heart torn apart, but it does reduce the possibility or the impact. I'm not sure if I was dealing with a fearful avoidant, dismissive avoidant, or narcissistic behaviors in my relationships, or just flat-out selfishness. Or if I just completely lacked all boundaries and self-respect. Either way my love stories have been hard and have ended in disappointment and heartbreak.

While I was married, many times my willingness to continue, fix, or move forward was about maintaining our family unit. It wasn't about fixing us, the couple, or the love story. Being with my former husband, I believe my patience became better. It was a result of him and his family having priority over me.

That better level of patience allowed me to be so, so very patient with the Marine. My Ex-Husband and I raised a family together despite the disease of alcoholism. So, I am sure that there will be opportunities that I will see him again. My Ex-Marine on the other hand, I just may never see him again in this lifetime. In the case of the Marine, I sacrificed what I wanted for myself in our relationship. I didn't fully see how much I contorted myself for him until after the heartbreak. I suppressed my desires to not pressure or overwhelm him. So, I repeatedly chose to go along and put my own needs aside. I knew what my needs were and with him stating he wanted us to remain together, I had been the prime opportunity in which I should have stood up for myself and said what I needed from him at the time. If he wasn't willing to commit, I should have continued my search for a place in which I would be alone.

With him, I was possibly holding on to who I thought he was, just to find out that version in my head just wasn't true. That version of who I believed him to be, maybe just wasn't real. I suppose this is me removing him from the pedestal I placed him on. A man of maturity and integrity would have not been able to do what he has done. So, I suppose he jumped off the pedestal. In reality, the Marine never showed he should be in that position. My expectations were too high for him. I have to be accountable for thinking he was better than he was.

In my sentimental heart, I would want to see him one more time. The love of my life that betrayed me once again. To look into his eyes and touch his face again. That is the sentimental, romantic me. The hard-core, stiff backbone me would like to touch his face. Just not gently in any way.

I believe life is easier when there are people around you who love and care for you. There have been times since this has happened where I have questioned myself as to why he didn't love me and why he didn't fight for us. I have questioned myself as to why some men look at me and feel as though they need to humble me somehow. Or to attempt to make me feel as though whatever my accomplishments or looks are, they are not enough. It is so easy to feel as though we are not measuring up to a standard when someone you love doesn't choose to love you properly in return.

A large part of the process of healing is recognizing that some people absolutely do not care about any pain that they may inflict on others. With that being true, the probability of ever receiving any type of apology is likely nonexistent. So, it is important to be able to recognize that healing doesn't require an acknowledgement of wrongs, or an apology from the offender. The reality is that if individuals behaved more accountably to their own actions, they are less likely to inflict harm towards others in the first place. So, it is important to know that an apology most likely will never be given. The most important part of healing is learning to forgive yourself. Forgiving yourself, for not protecting yourself better. For not paying attention to possible signs that something was wrong. Forgiving yourself for your part in any of the problems.

For my love stories, I have had to learn to forgive myself for not following the voice of God when I heard it and not using my discernment. I've had to forgive myself for putting others' needs before myself in situations that allowed others to take my intentions for granted and personal detriment. Learning not to bulldoze over incidents and issues, but to take note of things and being accountable. Healing is a battle. It is a battle for you, that maybe is fighting against a piece of you. It is an emotional battle, that you have to choose you every time! As important as trust is, there is a such thing as trusting too much. I believe I have been guilty of that. Trust but verify, is a saying for a reason. Trusting blindly is a flaw, and I have to do better with that.

Oftentimes people treat break-ups as not being a big deal. Maybe there are times when they aren't and other times they are devastating. Heartbreak has the potential to taint a person's entire view of intimacy, love, trust, and relationships. I don't regret giving the love and patience that I have given because they may have really needed it at the time. I gave my best and now I have to leave it all behind. I have to continuously choose me. Without a shadow of a doubt My Ex-husband and my Ex-Marine have been a blessing to me and as well as I to them. I always attempted to be a Queen in their lives. There is more than one type of Queen. I am not the Queen that is limited by my beauty, charm, and comfort. I am the type of Queen that is willing and able to fight alongside my

King or to pick up the sword of my King and fight to protect him if necessary. All Queens are not the same!

In the case of My Ex-husband, I was the Queen Elizabeth of that relationship. My role required me to maintain the kingdom (household) without the guidance and luxury of having a king. He remained a Prince and seemingly refused to ever take the mantle of King at home. With the relationship with the Marine, I would say that he was the King of our kingdom; however, for whatever reason he didn't like the power I wielded as his Queen. I held power too. Somewhere along the line, he didn't see the value in my strengths or maybe saw them as a threat to him. He no longer saw the values within me and possibly saw the other style queen more advantageous or simpler to control. I recognize the importance of knowing your own power.

These experiences have led me to a point in which the looming question presented itself again, "Am I enough?" Heartbreak has you questioning if you are deserving of love or maybe even thinking "what is wrong with me?" Or even, "why doesn't anyone want to love and treat me with respect?" It is so painful when these thoughts cloud your mind.

It's time for me to really be loved. I have experienced the worst of the worst of people that claimed to have loved me. I recognize that I deserve to be treated the way I have treated people, which has been with kindness, patience, empathy, and love. I deserve to be loved the right way. The world has taken so much from me. I too deserve to be loved and treated right in a manner that is consistent and unashamed for me the way I have shown up for people. I deserve that too. I matter too.

    A friend said to me that my Marine knew that I was vulnerable since I was coming out of a divorce. I don't necessarily disagree with that because although the divorce was recent, the marriage had been severed for years. By the time the divorce process had begun, there were no marital feelings to resolve. I would say that I was vulnerable as a person that had opened myself up to loving another person. I recognize that to truly love anyone, you have to become vulnerable to a certain level. Remember, I believe that love comes in several forms. Love for family, love for friends, love for partners, can all be slightly different. Being realistic, there is even a love for colleagues and co-workers. Intimate love requires vulnerability. However true love requires a level deeper than intimacy. True love requires the vulnerability to have a willingness to show your soul to the other person and accept their soul as well.

True love and friendship must be mutual.

True love is when someone is there for you, no matter if times are good or bad. Sometimes hard and sometimes easy.

People don't get to critique how I am hurt, or how much I hurt after they are the ones to have hurt me.

My love stories have been blessings to me, and I have been blessings to them even though they did not conclude with a happy ending. Love stories are not written by a singular author, it requires two willing hearts.

Even with it being unexpected it was in its purest form of greatness. I recognize I chose the men that were part of my love stories. In the end they just didn't choose to love me in return.

In easy and hard times, we choose to love or not. Love is a choice every day.

Is there love out there for me? I don't know. I wish for myself, that someone, one day will actually truly love me again and will work towards doing their part so that it is forever. I believe and trust that if God has made me with this desire in my heart to love and be loved, there is someone who is made to be able to love me. I look forward to love finding me again. I will welcome love back into my life. Someone who loves and accepts me for who I am. For me, I understand how important it is to be the priority and "their" choice, without faltering.

My greatest love came to me when I wasn't looking for it and it was unexpected both times. I want grand gestures. Not necessarily public gestures, but sincere, loved out loud gestures.

We all reap what we sow.

I didn't deserve the betrayal and hurt that has been inflicted upon me. I deserve to love as deeply and thoroughly as I am able to love. The pain that I have endured has been deliberate and intentional. Behaviors that were wrong and malicious.

Loving someone for who they are and where they are is still important. However, holding boundaries for yourself, getting what you need as well, is just as important.

I now recognize that being the love of my own life is what is best for me.

I choose peace. I choose love. I choose happiness. Today, I chose myself.

"What is for me will not pass me by and if it passes me by, it is not for me."

Revenge of a Broken Heart

TL Phillips